D1571406

CONTENTS

FOREWORD

In my ministry at First Presbyterian Church in San Antonio, Texas, one of my great privileges was to teach a weekly bible study. Every Wednesday I reviewed, with the small group leaders, the questions for the assigned passage of Scripture. For the last decade or so of my tenure at the church, Susan Kerr hosted these leaders in her home. It was there that I learned about, but never saw, her beloved dogs, Spencer and Bridget (about whom you will soon read). She had discreetly placed the dogs out of sight in another room. The group was never small because her leadership and spiritual insight were a magnet to those who recognized the authenticity of her life and faith.

After retirement from the church, I continued to teach as Professor of Pastoral Leadership at Austin Presbyterian Theological Seminary. Susan's group would not consider giving up their Bible study and Susan agreed to continue the study at her home. Through word of mouth the group grew to over fifty participants, and they moved to a neighbor's larger house. These gatherings were the genesis of *Intersections of Grace: Reflections on a Life of Faith.* Before the weekly study began, Susan would stand before this large group of women from a variety of Protestant and Catholic traditions and experiences and deliver a short talk, a reflection on faith. These talks were based on God-given insights from nature, travel, pets, and literature that she could apply to the topic of the weekly study.

Because the design of the Professor Chair at the seminary was for six years, I was wondering what I would do when my term ended. Wondered, until one day I ran into

Susan at a hardware store. We talked about her group, and she said, "Why don't you become our teacher? You choose the Scripture." I accepted her invitation and thus began two years as the privileged teacher of this wonderful group of ladies. But Susan never gave her talk when I was present. She waited until I had left and then she delivered her much anticipated "fireside chat."

I had been told by others about them but never was I in the listening audience—her humility forbade my being a listener—until several months ago she presented me with a sampling of these marvelous essays and asked my reflection and opinion.

My response was immediate. I wrote, "Susan, such a gift you have and how well you used it. These meditations that you shared are touching, inspiring, challenging, comforting, moving, and very real. They come out of your life, and your experiences, and your deep faith. Your use of Scripture, poetry, songs, movies, literature, and hymns is particularly significant and helpful in moving the reader to share your experience, and they all cause the reader to think and meditate."

I am honored to have a voice in commending these compelling reflections. Susan's words and images, her verbs and powerful adjectives enable the reader to experience Susan's joy of life lived in the "grip of grace." The reality of God's great love is made accessible in each of these meditations.

To God Be the Glory.

Louis H. Zbinden, Jr.

The Louis H. and Katherine S. Zbinden Professor of Pastoral Ministry and Leadership Emeritus, Austin Presbyterian Theological Seminary

INTRODUCTION

In 2004, several friends and I decided to organize an in-home Bible study, open to women of varying ages and church affiliations, Protestant and Catholic, some with little connection to a church. Having been a small group leader in a Bible study at First Presbyterian Church in San Antonio, Texas for many years, this was something new for me. Soon after starting this study—which grew to over fifty participants and lasted seven years—I began to give a short devotional talk at the beginning of each week's study, which someone dubbed "Susan's fireside chats." A number of the women encouraged me to transform my speaking notes into written essays, compiled here as *Intersections of Grace*.

Many of these devotionals were inspired by our pets, our summer home in the Blue Ridge Mountains, nature, travel—and of course, by the word of God. Although God speaks to us in unique and individual ways, I *hear* him best through the visual. As a lover of photography, I find that looking through the lens of a camera sharpens my focus on the ways God intersects the paths of our daily lives, if we're paying attention. My photographs—some of which are included here—have been a source of inspiration and a subject for meditative prayer. A cemetery of wooden crosses and bright flowers, a tree of thorns, a single orange poppy in a sea of green wheat, stone steps on an ancient church in Sicily—all became pictures of a walk of faith for me.

In the photo on the cover of this book, the road disappears into the distance, a destination unknown. The road led ultimately to an intersection. We had to make a choice. Do we stop or yield? Do we continue in the same direction, go back the way we came, or turn right or left? Because we made the correct choice, we finally arrived at a house in the Italian countryside called *Ben Contento*, a place of rest, refreshment, and reunion with friends and family.

Each of us is traveling on a road with God, who accompanies us and intersects our path. We can, however, be like the travelers on the road to Emmaus who failed to recognize that it was Jesus walking beside them, too preoccupied with the events of the day to notice God in their midst. Looking back on my life, I see God's ever present grace. I also see how frequently I ran the red light at those intersections and kept traveling on at full speed. Finally, at a difficult point in my life in my early thirties, I did stop to notice and chose to yield to his plans for my life. I realized that he had been waiting for me to accept his invitation to a place of *Ben Contento*, a place of rest, refreshment, and time to enjoy the company of fellow travelers.

As the ancient Israelites wandered in the wilderness, they received two seemingly contradictory instructions—move forward *and* stand still. My hope is that these essays will invite you into some standing-still times and then to move forward with God as your walking partner, alert to intersections of grace that crisscross our paths with the power to renew, restore, and transform our lives.

Susan Kerr

INTERSECTIONS OF GRACE

REFLECTIONS ON A LIFE OF FAITH

ONE

LIMOGES BOXES

Where can I go from your Spirit? Where can I flee from your presence? . . .
If I rise on the wings of the dawn, if I settle on the far side of the sea
even there . . . your hand will hold me fast.
—Psalm 139: 7–10

Thou art within me, behind, above—I will be thine because
I may and must.
—George MacDonald[1]

Europeans became fascinated with porcelain and ceramics as a result of Marco Polo's twenty-four-year trip to the Orient. It was believed that the white clay kaolin, the most important ingredient in porcelain, did not exist outside the Far East. When the clay was discovered in France in the mid-eighteenth century, the first porcelain box factory was soon established in the city of Limoges. These small hand-painted, hinged boxes soon became popular with the French aristocracy—and collecting them continues to this day.

My fascination with small boxes began when I was a child. At my mother's dressing table was a heart-shaped silver box that held two tiny baby shoes. My father's—a white bootie with his initials in pale blue: LJM; my mother's—pink quilted with white fur around the edge. Were my parents ever that small?

At an early age, I began my collection of porcelain Limoges boxes. A new one, a birthday present from my Aunt Jane, was recently added to the collection. It is a wrapped gift box, white with red hearts, a red bow on the top. When I placed it with the others on the coffee table, I spent time looking at these delicate creations, marveling at the variety of subjects– animals, flowers, fruits, and musical instruments. Shopping for a gift to mark a special occasion or event is easy. From birth to graduation to marriage, there is an appropriate design.

The pieces of my Limoges collection almost frame my life story: a box for a child's first lost tooth, a Bible when I was confirmed. An Eiffel Tower reminds me of a trip to Europe with my parents, a leopard for my first trip to Africa, a diploma for graduation from college. A wedding cake for our marriage in 1977. A stork for my first pregnancy. A pacifier for the birth of our daughter. Our interest in music is shown by a Limoges box of a grand piano, another of a guitar. A box of a pair of shoes that a friend gave me when I became a Christian—to symbolize that I would be the hands and feet of Christ. Boxes for the pets we have loved—a Cavalier King Charles Spaniel, a parrot, a rabbit, and numerous cats. Boxes to help me remember special holidays and celebrations—a pumpkin, a turkey, candy canes, and crèches. A Limoges box in the shape of a champagne cork purchased to celebrate our thirty-fifth anniversary.

Recently, I started giving Limoges boxes to my own children. A red London bus and the White House to symbolize our daughter's move from London to Washington, D.C. A box with a wedding cake with bride and groom for my recently married son and daughter-in-law. The variety is endless. There are not coffee tables large enough to chronicle our lives. From the perspective of hindsight and the blessing of faith, I realize that at each of these significant occasions and turning points, God was present, filling every moment, blessing every occasion. "That all things thou dost fill, I well may think."[2] George MacDonald's diary entry goes on to say, "Thy power doth reach me in so many ways."

Regardless of our occupation, education, profession, training, or experience, God will meet us right where we are. God knows us individually: our talents, gifts, quirks, interests, and personalities. He never resorts to "mass-producing" copies.[3] Because the God who never changes knows that we are constantly changing, he lets himself be known by over 300 names in Scripture. As we change in mood, circumstance, priority, or perspective, we may gravitate to a different name of God than we did yesterday or last week or ten years ago. The Limoges boxes on my coffee table name the ages and stages of my life—childhood, faith, travel, marriage, parenthood, anniversaries, passions, and interests. And, for every one of these, God was there with a name of his own.

- If I were a gardener, he would be my rose of Sharon.
- If I were a sculptor, he would be my rock.
- If I were a soldier, he would be my shield.
- If I were a builder, he would be my strong foundation.

PRAYER

Father, as I hold each of the boxes in my hand and reflect on the stages of my life that they represent, I am filled with gratitude that you were there. Each moment, each change, each circumstance was full of your presence, your grace, your touch, and your blessing. You have been a Father to me, while at other times drawing alongside as a friend. In difficult times, you have been my shield, fortress, and hiding place. In times of exhaustion and stress you have been my resting place. At times my darkness has cried out for your light, times when the night was long and I yearned for you as the bright Morning Star. There are more "Limoges boxes" to come. Help me to expect your presence in my future and in the future of my loved ones.

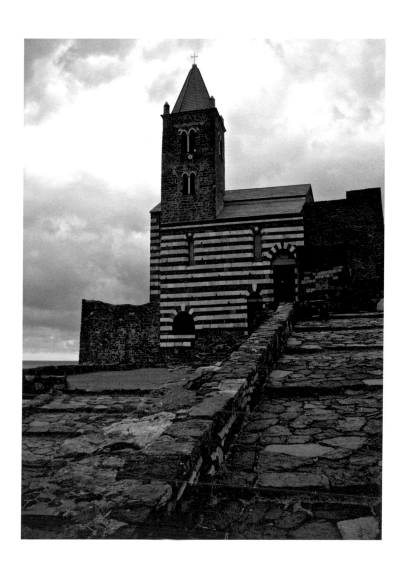

THE TOUCH OF GRACE

Perverse and foolish, oft I strayed, but, yet in love he sought me; and on his shoulder gently laid, and home, rejoicing, brought me.
—Henry W. Baker[4]

Our lives are touched by God's grace from our birth to our death. As Christians, our future holds the promise of an "inheritance that can never perish, spoil or fade. This inheritance is kept in heaven for [us] . . ." (1 Pet. 1:4). Perhaps we should have only one word on our tombstone: KEPT.

God's grace offers the hope and possibility that our lives can be transformed, here and now. "Before and after" testimonies demonstrate that faith in Christ and the power of the indwelling Holy Spirit make a difference where the rubber meets the road—in how we live our daily lives and how we respond to pain and suffering.

Because Peter was touched and transformed by grace, his story is a before and after story. In the Gospel accounts we see Peter as a "wishy-washy, mollycoddling, shilly-shally man."[5] However, after he had encountered the resurrected Christ and received the Holy Spirit at Pentecost, Peter had grown into his Christ-given name: "Rock Man." In the book of Acts, he continues to preach about Christ's death and resurrection despite threats and warnings from the religious authorities. Even in prison, he endured persecution with boldness, courage, and even joy.

In Peter's first epistle, he speaks of faith being tested to prove that it is genuine. He had faced a crucible of faith when he denied and disowned Jesus, the man he had loved and followed for three years, the one he had confessed as being the Christ. Peter failed the test even though Jesus had prayed for his faith to stand firm. Jesus had told Peter to pray so he would not fall into temptation. He fell. After vehemently saying he would never desert Jesus, he just as vehemently denied ever knowing him.

When the rooster crowed after Peter's third denial, Jesus "turned and looked straight at Peter" (Lk. 22:61). To imagine what Peter must have felt at that moment we would need to multiply by one hundred times our own greatest guilt, regret, or shame. The look in Jesus' eyes surely conveyed sadness and disappointment, but also love and understanding.

A few days later, over a breakfast of fish with his risen Lord, Peter's failure was overshadowed by a great forgiveness. But in the time between Peter's denial of Christ and his forgiveness on the shore of the Sea of Galilee, he must have done a lot of remembering. Using our sanctified imagination, let's enter Peter's mind:

> I'll never forget my brother Andrew's excitement when he came running to find me on the beach, saying, "We have found the Messiah!" When I first met Jesus, he changed my name from Simon to Cephas or "Rock," a name that suggests strength, changelessness, resolution, and durability. I have failed to live up to the potential he saw in me.
>
> There were a few times when the name Rock was appropriate for me. After my audacious request to walk on the water, I took my eyes off Jesus and began to sink—like a rock. Jesus once called me a stone, actually a stumbling stone, because I disputed his assertion that he had to suffer and die. And the night I denied knowing him, I felt that my heart had turned to stone, "shattered so

mercilessly that among its pieces not a fragment [could] be found . . ." (Isa. 30:14). So much for living up to my new name!

I keep asking myself, How could I? after all the things I had seen and heard.

How could I? I had witnessed the miracles, heard his teaching, been awed by the authority with which he drove the money changers out of the Temple and confronted the religious leaders.

How could I? I had seen his power over nature when he calmed the storm.

How could I? I had seen his power when he raised Lazarus from the dead.

How could I? I had witnessed him speaking with Moses and Elijah, "his clothes . . . as bright as a flash of lightening" (Lk. 9:29).

How could I? I had seen the anguish of his soul as he prayed face down on the ground in the Garden of Gethsemane.

How could I? I had heard the testimony of others. John the Baptist called him the Lamb of God who takes away the sin of the world. The Samaritan villagers had recognized him as the Savior of the world. And I myself had understood that he was the holy one of God with the words of eternal life. It was after I proclaimed his identity that he promised me the keys to the kingdom of heaven.

Some of Jesus' words torment me: "Whoever wants to save their life will lose it" (Mt. 16:25); "What good is it for someone to gain the whole world, yet forfeit their soul?" (Mk. 8:36); "If anyone is ashamed of me and my words . . . the Son of Man will be ashamed of them when he comes in his Father's glory with the holy angels" (Mk. 8:38). I disowned Jesus to save my life. Have I lost him forever? Are the keys to the Kingdom no longer mine? Are the doors to the Kingdom forever locked?

The town of Portovenere, on the Mediterranean coast of Tuscany, is known as the sixth village of the Cinque Terra. On its rocky promontory stands the Church of San Pietro, a weather vane of a rooster on its roof. The bronze doors of the church depict the story of God's grace. Because this is the church of Saint Peter, it is really the story of God's grace in Peter's life, but God's grace is always a universal story, so it is our story also.

On the bottom panel of the left door is a small representation of a cock crowing, the audible confirmation of Jesus' prediction of Peter's denial. In the middle of the door is the figure of Peter, every muscle in his body taut, as he struggles and strains, his arms stretched toward God, whose image is at the top of the door. Peter is trying to reach God, trying with all his effort to close the distance that separates them. In all likelihood, Peter heard a rooster crow every morning for the rest of his life. Was he ever free of remorse and guilt? The other door answers this question.

On the bottom panel of the right door is a basket of fish, a reminder that on the shore of the Sea of Galilee, over a breakfast of fish, Jesus let Peter know that he was still needed for the work of the Kingdom: "feed my lambs." The striking figure on this door is not the struggling Peter, but the figure of God, leaning over with his arms outstretched as he places in Peter's open hand the keys of the Kingdom.

The left door represents Peter's and our condition without the touch of grace. We have all heard the rooster crow. We have all sinned and know that it separates us from the fellowship and relationship God desires to have with us. Our upward reach to God—all our striving to do better, to be better, and all of our resolutions to improve—will not bridge that separation.

God's grace is always reaching out to us ". . .in our low estate" (Ps. 136:23). He takes the initiative to reach down from heaven to take our hand. Grace is the hand of God that continues to lead and guide us, his hand not withdrawn when we have sinned. By the grace of "the Inescapable God," we are assured of his nearness even when we have made our bed in Sheol.

When the doors of San Pietro are closed, the depiction of the rooster and the basket of fish are almost touching. In the same way that:

- Our failure is touched by God's forgiveness.
- Our shame is touched by his salvation.
- Our guilt is touched by his grace.
- Our remorse is touched by his redemption.

In his book *In the Grip of Grace*, Max Lucado reminds his readers to do more than dip their toes into God's pool of mercy. We must plunge in and accept God's full cleansing and forgiveness.

Peter plunged in, literally. Will you? In Peter's epistle, the new man, the "Rock Man", writes of a new life and a new hope. He has found both. With open hands, we will receive the touch of grace so that when the rooster crows, it will no longer be a reminder of guilt and shame, but just another of God's creatures heralding the beginning of a new day.

PRAYER

God of grace, we thank you that we are still "kept" in spite of our failures and denials. We claim your promise that our future inheritance is safe, that the doors to the Kingdom are open. We thank you for the possibility of transformation and renewal so that we too may have a testimony of "before and after."

THREE

ROAD TRIP

If your presence does not go with us, do not send us up from here.
How will anyone know that you are pleased with me and
with your people unless you go with us?
—Exodus 33:15–16

We all remember car trips when we were kids in the 1950s, back in the day when Dinah Shore sang "See the USA in your Chevrolet!" No seat belts, no air conditioning. Stacks of new comic books did not prevent complaining. It was too hot, the radio produced only static, our legs were stuck to the plastic seat covers or scratched by wool upholstery. The hours were interminable—especially if your father stopped to read every historical marker along the highway. The perennial question of the trip—"How much farther?" We cared nothing about the journey. We were only interested in the destination, the Howard Johnson's. A swim in the motel pool, shrimp cocktail, and blueberry ice cream were our rewards for enduring another boring day on the road.

The Israelites endured a forty-year-long road trip with God as they journeyed from Egypt to the Promised Land. Moses had asked Pharaoh to "let my people go" so they could celebrate "a festival to me in the wilderness" (Exod. 5:1). While on the journey, they grumbled and complained, lamenting that slavery in Egypt was preferable to wandering aimlessly in the wilderness. As God's chosen people, who had been delivered from slavery "with an outstretched arm and with mighty acts of judgment" (Exod. 6:6), they wondered why the journey had to be so long and so difficult. Why didn't God take them on the shortest, most direct route? But God knew they needed all the days of the journey to learn to follow him, to obey him, and to trust him. In the midst of God's goodness and provision, they were not exactly celebrating on the way—because they were destination people, eager to arrive in the land of milk and honey. How much farther?

One October, my husband John and I took a grown-up road trip from Washington, D.C., to our family home in North Carolina. Air conditioning, leather seats, and satellite radio kept complaining to a minimum. Crossing the bridge at Annapolis, we arrived on the Delmarva Peninsula that lies between the Chesapeake Bay and the Atlantic Ocean. Del-Mar-Va is comprised of three states—Delaware, Maryland, and Virginia. Who in the world established those state boundaries? Maybe this is a new way to describe the Trinity to someone—one peninsula made up of three different states, each with its own character, history, and government.

Heading south on the Delmarva Peninsula from the Eastern Shore of Maryland, we passed Pleasure House Road before entering a long stretch through the Great Dismal Swamp. There was no quick exit, the only option was to continue driving through it. When would we emerge from this depressing place? I looked at the map hoping to find the promise of something more positive beyond the Swamp. And there it was right on the map: Wildlife *Refuge*, and the towns Sandy *Cross*, and New *Hope*.

The tip of the Delmarva Peninsula is a tiny part of Virginia, separated from the mainland by a twenty-mile tunnel/bridge that goes over (and under) the Chesapeake. The bridge is only about thirty feet above the rough water. A nor'easter that was blowing in made it feel as if a huge wave might engulf us at any minute, a strong wind might blow our car over the railing. When we were in the tunnel, we were eager to emerge again into the light. Contrasts confronted us: a group of dolphins frolicking in the heavy swells, and three dead seagulls—blown onto the bridge by the high winds.

After a succession of one-night stays, I woke up in the dark of night wondering, "Where am I?" St. Michaels, Maryland? Edenton, North Carolina? Winston-Salem? My memory was already vague about where we had been, the roads we had traveled. I was no longer appreciating the scenery outside the window because of my eagerness to reach our destination; I was forgetting to celebrate the journey.

Our journey on the road reveals a lot about human nature, about life, and about God. Whether the traveler is a kid in the back seat of her parents' car, an adult couple, or thousands of Israelites, there are some common truths.

We prefer the smooth road, the shortest route—grumbling and complaining if the trip is too long or too difficult. In our determination to reach our destination quickly—the Ho-Jo, the Holy Land, North Carolina, or an easier time in our life—we can forget to enjoy the scenery of the moment. When we find ourselves driving in the Dismal Swamp, we want to accelerate through it, or at least find a detour or short cut. What we really want is an intersection with Pleasure House Road. But God tells us the same thing he told the Israelites—go forward (Exod. 14:15), keep moving in the dismal times of our lives—remembering that we have the promise of the cross, the comfort of safe refuge in our Savior, and the hope of new beginnings. Can we celebrate the journey?

We yearn for clear guidance from God while we are on the road. Perhaps a visible sign of God's presence like the one given to the Israelites: a cloud and a pillar of fire, and a parting of the sea. I wish God's directions were as clear as those we got from our GPS in the rental car. "Turn right, straight ahead, wrong turn, go the other way." GPS! GOD PLEASE SHOW! Show us your path, your plan, your purpose. GPS. God Please Show us that your presence is before us, behind us, and beside us as we travel on our way. Then maybe we can celebrate the journey.

The journey teaches us that life is full of contrasts: dead seagulls and dancing dolphins. Lemons and lemonade. The Dismal Swamp and Pleasure House Road are parallel tracks, as we experience joy and sadness simultaneously. As my mother was dying in the hospital, a newborn baby was uttering gusty cries from the room next door. Birth, life, death. Baptisms, weddings, and funerals. Can we celebrate the journey?

You may wake in the night of difficult circumstances feeling dangerously close to the rough waters, buffeted by strong winds, desperate to see light at the end of the tunnel. And you may wonder, Where am I? How did I get here? Where am I going? Where is God? You try to find comfort in Scripture: God "will turn my wailing into dancing . . . weeping may stay for the night, but rejoicing comes in the morning" (Ps. 30:5,11). But like the impatient child in the back seat asking his father "How much farther?" we ask our heavenly Father, "How much farther?" When will I dance again? When will I get to the place of joy and gladness? God does not always take us the shortest way through difficulty. Like the Israelites, we need all the days of the journey to learn to follow him, obey him, and trust him.

Although we loved the clear directions from the GPS, the machine was not infallible. In the quaint town of Edenton, North Carolina, we entered the name Sean's Restaurant. The pleasant voice of the GPS responded "Sean's in Vermont?" "No!" we complained. We were too tired and hungry to travel any farther along this road. Half a block later, we found the restaurant.

When we ask God "How much farther?" the solution to our problem may come sooner than we think. His deliverance may be around the corner.

> ✣ It may be soon that you see light at the end of the tunnel.
> ✣ It may be soon that the violent winds are calm.
> ✣ It may be soon that you leave the Dismal Swamp and are driving on Pleasure House Road.
> ✣ It may be soon that you see dolphins dancing on waves.

PRAYER

L ord, the GPS gave us the option to choose the shortest route. That would always be our choice—the shortest route through suffering or pain. Some people have spent too much time in the Dismal Swamp and feel they are "wandering around the land in confusion, hemmed in by the desert" (Exod. 14:3). If you have lost sight of God's guidance for your future, it may be time to take a glance out of the rear view mirror and remember where you have been, roads already traveled. Reflect on what God has done for you in the past. Stop to read those historical markers by the roadside and see where he has guided you and accompanied you on your journey. And even though the road always calls you to move forward, remember the promise given to the Israelites as they began their wilderness journey: "The Lord will fight for you; you need only to be still" (Exod. 14:14). And remember the slogan of the Greyhound Bus Company: "Leave the driving to us." Sit back and trust that the future is held in God's strong hand. And, don't forget to celebrate the journey.

FOUR

THE POETRY OF GOD

Where were you when I laid the earth's foundation? . . .
while the morning stars sang together and all the angels shouted for joy . . .
when I made the clouds its garment and wrapped it in thick darkness.
—Job 38:4–9

God's written Word comes to us in many forms—history, narrative, law, prophecy, and wisdom sayings. And poetry, which comprises one-third of the Old Testament. I selected and arranged the following verses from Isaiah and Job, which is the longest poem of Scripture. They speak of God's sovereign power in creating the universe and his personal and immediate care over his creation. Read these verses and find rest for your soul.

I marked off the dimensions of the Earth
And laid its foundation.
I stretched a measuring line across it
And laid its cornerstone.
I have held the dust of the earth in a basket
And have weighed the mountains on a scale.
I comprehend its vast expanses.
While the morning stars sang together
And all the angels shouted for joy,
I gave orders to the morning

And showed the dawn its place.
I have measured the waters in the hollow
    of my hand.
I shut the sea behind doors
Fixing its limits.
This is where your proud waves will halt.
I have journeyed to the springs of the sea
And walked in the recesses of the deep.
I know the way to the abode of light
And I know where the darkness resides;
I enter the storehouse of the snow and hail,
I cut a channel for the torrents of rain
And a path for the thunderstorm.
I water the desert where no man lives
To satisfy a desolate wasteland
And make it sprout with grass.
I am the Father of the rain and the drops of dew.
I tip over the water jars of the heavens
When the dust of earth becomes hard and the
    clods of earth stick together.
I give birth to the frost from the heavens.
I bring out the starry host one by one and call
    them each by name,
And bring forth the constellations in their season.
I bind the beautiful Pleiades
And cut loose the cords of Orion.
I lead out the Bear with its cubs.
I established the laws of Heaven
And set up my dominion over the earth.
I count the clouds and wear them as my garment.
I raise my voice to the clouds
And send lightning bolts on their way.
I hunt the prey for the lions to satisfy their
    hunger
As they crouch in their dens or lie in wait in a
    thicket.
I provide food for the raven when its young cry
    out to me.
I know when the mountain goats give birth

And watch when the doe bears her fawn.
I count the months till they bear and know the
    time they give birth.
The hawk takes flight by my wisdom
And the eagle soars at my command.
I tend my flock like a shepherd;
I gather my lambs in my arms and carry them
    close to my heart.
I give strength to the weary
And increase the power of the weak.
You can renew your strength by putting your
    hope in me.
You will soar on wings like eagles,
You will run and not grow weary,
You will walk and not be faint.
I carry you on the wings of eagles
To bring you to myself.

PRAYER

The God-breathed-word comes to us in such eloquence and beauty. Let us pray for those whose hearts remain hard even after encountering such powerful words. Open their eyes and touch their hearts by the life-giving force of your ways and your thoughts that are so much higher than our own.

FIVE

CLOUDS' ILLUSIONS

*Now faith is confidence in what we hope for and assurance
about what we do not see.*

—Hebrews 11:1

For thirty years, our family has spent part of each summer in the Blue Ridge Mountains of North Carolina. On the twenty-one-hour drive from Texas to North Carolina, anticipation builds as we pass familiar landmarks—the Atchafalaya Swamp, the bridge over the Mississippi River, the giant peach in Gaffney, South Carolina. Driving the last sixteen miles on a winding mountain road we see a sign that indicates we have just crossed the Continental Divide. At the small post office we turn on the road that will take us to our house. Our tradition is that all the windows are rolled down and every head, human and canine, leans out to inhale the distinctive scent of mountain laurel, pine, and rhododendron. Back at last! We have been homesick for eleven months.

The Blue Ridge Mountains are old mountains, part of the Appalachian chain. Worn down by centuries of wind, rain, and erosion, they are gentle blue folds, not at all like the Rockies. The words of John Calvin's hymn come to mind, "Thou hast the true and perfect gentleness, no harshness hast thou . . ." When the light of the moon illuminates the mountain ridges, you can almost imagine that you are on a ship in the ocean on a choppy sea.

When I get up in the morning and open the curtains, I hope for a clear day. On those mornings, I go outside with a cup of coffee, our dog Spencer, and my Bible. When I see Venus in the eastern sky, I reflect on one of the names of Jesus, "the Bright Morning Star" (Rev. 22:16), the herald of a new day, signaling the dawn of hope and joy.

On these clear mornings, I am inspired to worship. The grandeur of God's creation reminds me of his might and power. A pearl-studded spider web and a tiny hummingbird remind me of his attention to the small details of nature. I love the mountain solitude. So did Jesus.

The 180-degree panorama from our house reminds me that God has "removed my sins from him, as far as the east is from the west" (Ps. 103:12). I have my bearings on a clear day, a long perspective because of the view that extends fifty miles beyond our back porch. The tall peak in the distance is Fisher's in Virginia; the gentle rise straight ahead is Mt. Airy, the inspiration for Mayberry, the town in *The Andy Griffith Show*. To the east is the distinctive shape of Pilot Mountain, outside Winston-Salem, where our daughter attended college.

Although I love clear days in North Carolina, I am accustomed to sudden changes in the mountain weather. The fog will come. Sometimes it comes gradually, beginning with small wisps of smoke in the valley that climb up the mountain and float through the window screens, settling in the living room like an uninvited guest.

> The fog comes
> on little cat feet.
>
> It sits looking
> over harbor and city
> on silent haunches
> and then moves on.[6]

At other times the fog suddenly envelops the mountain, making me feel trapped inside a fluffy white marshmallow. To relieve the monotony of socked-in days, we would take our young children to the front lawn of the inn where they delighted in playing hide-and-seek in the fog—two tow-headed children disappearing into the white mist.

On foggy days, the familiar shapes and contours of my beloved mountains are hidden. My landmarks, my orientation, my long perspective have vanished. Gone is my inspiration to worship.

Driving in the fog is a challenge. It is impossible to anticipate the bends and turns on the mountain road. Proceeding slowly, head leaning out of the window, I strain to see the yellow stripe, which is my path, my guide, and my hope of reaching my destination safely. I am eager for the fog to lift.

In the same way, I long for clear days with God, days when I have my bearings, a good perspective, a view of what he is doing in my life. I want to see clearly the yellow stripe of his will and guidance as I am confronted with decisions and choices. Is the road ahead smooth and straight or should I prepare for bumps, curves, and sudden turns? Am I on the right path, headed for the destination he has in mind? We are not comfortable with ambiguity or mystery, wanting God to give us clarity about his purposes and plans as we travel the stages of our life journey.

We coin phrases like "seeing is believing," "I'll believe it when I see it," "out of sight, out of mind." This is not always God's way. Through the biblical writers, we are encouraged to change our perspective: "faith is confidence in what we hope for and assurance about what we do not see" (Heb. 11:1); "What is seen is temporary, what is not seen is eternal" (2 Cor. 4:18); "For we live by faith, not by sight" (2 Cor. 5:7); "hope that is seen is no hope at all" (Rom. 8:24); "blessed are those who have not seen and yet have believed" (Jn. 20:29).

But a fog can descend in our souls, blocking the clarity we desire in our spiritual life. A "cloud of unknowing"[7] can cause our vision of God to be hazy, his activity in our lives difficult to understand or discern. Did the disciples feel that way in their exhaustion and fear in the stormy night on the Sea of Galilee? "Where is he? Does he know we are in danger? Does he care? Will he save us? When?" We may ask the same questions when we are caught in a storm and feel the darkness closing in. Just as my view of the mountains is obscured by the fog, we may no longer see the "Mount of God's unchanging love."[8] The clouds keep us from seeing the breadth of his mercy, the familiar contours of his compassion. We seek him, but he seems to be hiding. Leonard Cohen's song "Both Sides Now" says that clouds "block the sun, they rain and snow on everyone." Spiritual fog can block our view of the SON.

One summer, a good friend came for her first visit to our mountain retreat, eager to see the view I had always raved about. Unfortunately, the fog visited as long as she did and she never saw the view. She joked that the view from our porch was probably just a Walmart or a used-car lot, skeptical because she had never seen what I had seen. But we are not first-time visitors to God's grace and mercy. We have seen the view. We know there is *Someone* out there beyond the fog. We must believe that even when we cannot see, the "Father is always at his work" (Jn. 5:17). Cohen's song continues: "I've looked at clouds from both sides now. But something's lost and something's gained in living every day." We must also look at clouds from both sides. It is often in the fog that we find God. It is often in the dark and stormy night that we become aware that he is in the boat, pulling the oars with us.

Perhaps we need a strategy for foggy days:

⋆ The temptation on foggy days is to "tuck in" and stay home. It feels safer. But sometimes we have to venture out. In the same way, when the fog descends on our lives, we may have to simply move forward, straining to find the yellow stripe of God's presence and guidance. We must get out of the house even when we don't have all the answers, even when we can't envision the road ahead.

- When you are driving in the fog, the sight of approaching headlights gives the assurance that you are not alone. That car has already traveled the road you are about to travel. Jesus is always our approaching light, and he has traveled every road ahead of you—the road of grief, loneliness, persecution, suffering, and even death.
- Better yet, find a car in front of you and follow its taillights. Follow the light of Christ. He will lead you to safety.
- In the fog, pray that other drivers have their headlights turned on. Be with other people of the light, your sisters and brothers in Christ.

Another phrase from Cohen's song: "It's clouds' illusions I recall, I really don't know clouds at all." The illusion of the mountain fog is that nothing exists beyond the back porch. The only reality is the impenetrable fog. The illusion of the cloud in our life with God would say:

- Beyond this problem, there is no solution.
- Beyond this sadness, there is no happiness.
- Beyond this confusion, there is no clarity.
- Beyond this sin, there is no forgiveness.
- Beyond this illness, there is no health.
- Beyond this death, there is no life.

PRAYER

If you are experiencing clear days, praise God. If the fog has descended on your soul, be confident it will lift. When your vision of God's plan, presence, or purpose is hazy, remember that you have seen the view. Don't listen to the voice of the skeptic who says God is not present in the midst of difficulty.

SIX

THE L'IMITATION OF GOD

Who has measured the waters in the hollow of his hand, or with the breadth of his hand marked off the heavens?

—Isaiah 40:12

Our Christmas was a little *off* one year. Instead of spreading Christmas cheer, we spread a virulent strain of the stomach virus, which struck every adult in our house, at two-day intervals. Because my husband, John, was sick on Christmas morning, we didn't open our gifts until evening, not our normal tradition. Christmas lunch was at my brother's house, as it has been for forty years, but my sister-in-law was in the hospital with pneumonia. Even the Christmas Eve service didn't work its usual magic. Singing "Silent Night" with hundreds of candles flickering in the cold December sky did not elicit the emotion I usually feel on this blessed evening.

Finally, December 29, I was overcome with emotion— a deep sadness that I had somehow missed Christmas. My expectations had been disappointed. Not typically a high-drama person, my emotions were intense. Fortunately, "all through the house, not a creature was stirring, not even a mouse."[9] Only God and our dog, Spencer, were awake to witness the scene. Spencer couldn't take it and removed himself to another room. God stayed. Kneeling in front of our beautiful Nativity scene, I wept. I removed the baby Jesus from the manger. The wise men turned their camels around and headed back east, as if saying, "There was no King in this house, no one to worship here." I cried harder. Unable to sleep, I decided it was time to take the decorations off the Christmas tree while listening to Handel's *Messiah*. I cried harder. Through my tears, I noticed an unopened present under the tree. What an ungrateful person! A gift purchased, with time and thought—and the box hadn't even been opened! And then I knew. I was the ungrateful one. The gift of Christ at Christmas, a costly gift purchased for me, with time and thought, and I had failed to open it.

I had left God in the box! God in a box? An absurd concept! Quite to the contrary, God has been doing things outside the box from the moment that a virgin became pregnant by the Holy Spirit, from the moment our King and Savior was born in a stable instead of a palace. And yet God's people, to whom the prophecies had been given, could not embrace the unexpected. Instead, they tried to keep the King in a box, bound by the limitations of their social conditions and cultural assumptions, bound by their religion, by their laws and traditions.

I am reminded of the Jack-in-the-Box toy that amused us when we were children. You turned the handle, never knowing when Jack would pop up. When he appeared, you squealed with delight and then pushed him back in the box so the whole process could start again. It was as if the religious leaders had been turning the handle for centuries, waiting for the Messiah to appear. But, when he did pop up, Jack did not look or behave according to expectations. Nor did he accomplish what they desired or in the manner they had anticipated. Because he was not the Messiah they expected—BAM. Back in the box! It was a little like my Christmas—high expectations that were disappointed.

The phrase "the limitation of Christ" has been in my mind for months. While I was reading Thomas à Kempis's book *The Imitation of Christ*, an accidental ink mark on the cover changed the title to "The L'Imitation of Christ." God in a box? Christ limited? How can it be? How can you limit the one who "has held the dust of the earth in a basket and measured the waters in the hollow of his hand"? (Isa. 40:12).

In my collection of Limoges porcelain boxes is one that looks like a gift box with a red bow on the top. I keep it near my Bible as a daily reminder to open the gift, to take God out of the box of my own expectations, knowledge, and experience. It serves as a reminder that although we can never limit God, we can limit our awareness of his presence, our ability to hear his voice, and our sensitivity to his activity in our lives. J. B. Phillips, the author of *Your God Is Too Small*, understood that we could, in fact, keep God small.

We can limit God by what we know or think we know about him. In the Gospels Jesus is known as rabbi, teacher, prophet, healer, miracle worker, son of Mary and Joseph, a man from Nazareth, sent from God, a man of learning, a good man. Because each of these is only a partial knowing of Jesus, they do limit him. God in the box with the lid partly open. Some knew him in a way that was totally wrong—demon-possessed, deceiver, blasphemer, only human. Only a few recognized Jesus' true identity: Son of God, Lamb of God, Savior of the world, and the one who was to come.

We can limit God by how we pray. Have you ever called a prayer meeting with God? You are the chairperson, of course. You call the meeting to order, go over your agenda, and perhaps have a PowerPoint presentation. When the meeting is adjourned (by you, of course), no one else has had a chance to speak—especially not God. You have told him what you want, when you want it accomplished, and arrogantly suggested how he might go about it. God in a box, indeed!

We limit God when we expect his answers to come in a specific way. One day I dialed 411 information, asking for Alamo Heights Chiropractic. The recorded reply— "Culpepper, Virginia?" "No, no, no!" I shouted into the phone. This was not the information I wanted and it made no sense! Are we willing to hear God speak out of the box? He speaks through his Word, through the words of others, through dreams and visions, and he speaks in the silence. When Jesus was ordered to keep his disciples from speaking, he said, "If they keep quiet, the stones will cry out" (Lk. 19:40). God's answers don't always come in the way we expect.

We can limit God by expecting his answers to come in our own timing, wrongly assuming that unanswered prayer means that God is not working in our circumstance, or even concerned. Henry David Thoreau writes of a night of heavy snowfall, a night so silent that one would assume that all has been quiet—the owl in his tree, the meadow mouse in his snug burrow, the rabbit, the squirrel, and the fox all housed. And then . . . in the morning "the myriad tracks in the snow remind us that each hour of the night is crowded with events, and the primeval nature [God] is still working and making tracks in the snow."[10]

We limit God if we confine him to a box labeled the past or the future. We remember past experiences, building little structures around our mountaintop moments, as Peter wanted to do at the Transfiguration. When we do this, we are neglecting to notice God's activity in the present. We may be holding God in reserve for a future time of crisis or suffering. That will be the time to draw near to him. We can also limit him to a time of day, a day in the week—a daily quiet time, church, or Bible study—forgetting to invite him to keep us company all day.

We can certainly limit God by our weak witness—too timid to speak because we aren't confident of our theology and feel we can't answer the tough questions.

God in a box? In the Old Testament, he really was in a box, his presence believed to be within the Ark of the Covenant, kept behind a curtain in the Holy of Holies, where only the high priest could enter once a year. With the incarnation, God stepped outside the box, literally. The gift was given. Will we open it?

In Victorian England, December 26 was set aside as "Boxing Day," a day to let the servants rest and to "box" up the leftover food and clothing to give to the poor. Let's not have 365 days of "boxing day" with God, an entire year when we keep him boxed up and limited by our idea of him, by how we pray, by looking for his answers to come only in our timing, or hearing his voice only in certain ways, or by encasing his presence in the past or saving him for the future.

With the Limoges box as a reminder, I resolve that this year, I will open the gift every day and let God out of the box.

THIS DAY, I will open the gift by what I know of God. I resolve to know him as sovereign, strong and steadfast in love. I will know him as faithful and good, a God of compassion who weeps over our suffering.

THIS DAY, I will open the gift by how I pray. With Mary and Martha as examples, I resolve to pray with their simplicity and trust, "Lord, the one you love is ill." I will lay my petitions before God, believing that all things are possible with him. I will try to leave the outcome in his hands knowing that the peace promised in Philippians 4:6–7 comes from giving him my requests and petitions, not in trying to accomplish the result on my own.

THIS DAY, I will open the gift by being patient with God's timing. If a prayer remains unanswered, I will trust that he has heard me, that he loves me and is working. I will trust that there are tracks in the snow on the silent night.

THIS DAY, I will open the gift by how I listen. When I don't hear his voice or discern his guidance, I will rely on the Holy Spirit to interpret my groanings that are too deep for words (Rom. 8:26) and to increase my ability to hear God's voice in the many different ways it may come. If God says "Culpepper, Virginia" in response to my "Alamo Heights Chiropractic," I will try to discern what he is trying to tell me. And I will give him moments of silence so he can speak.

THIS DAY, I will open the gift by pursuing the "Gospel of the Moment." Grateful for his involvement in the past and confident of his presence in the future, I will look for him in the ordinary activities of this present day.

THIS DAY, I will open the gift by my witness to others, remembering that this doesn't always require words, but can be accomplished with a smile or act of kindness. I will remember the example of John the Baptist and point to Jesus when I can. I will remember that a powerful testimony can be as simple as "I was blind but now I see!" (Jn. 9:25). I will remember that a woman of questionable reputation converted an entire town in Samaria. I will remember how easy it is to witness by saying "Merry Christmas" in response to every "Happy Holiday."

In mid-January, I am just beginning to open the gift of Christmas. The Nativity is still on the table in the entry hall. The baby Jesus is back in the manger; the wise men and their camels have returned. There is a King in this house; there is *Someone* to worship here. God is not limited; God is not in the box. Christ is alive, dwelling among us and surpassing the limits of our human imagination.

PRAYER

Jesus, you are the gift of Christmas, the gift that will keep giving all the months of the year. Let us be grateful recipients of this costly gift purchased for us, a gift that is fragile and needs to be handled with care. May we unwrap it daily so we can discover the richness of the treasure contained within. Let us not confine you within the limitation of our way of knowing you, our way of praying, our expectation of your timing, or your manner of intersecting our lives. Let us not limit you to the past or the future, but worship you now as our limitless God for whom all things are possible.

SEVEN

THE WALLS OF LUCCA

Though your riches increase, do not set your heart on them.
—Psalm 62:10

Walk about Zion, go around her, count her towers, consider well her ramparts,
view her citadels, that you may tell the next generation.
For this is our God forever and ever.
—Psalm 48:12–14

In October 2008, the global economy suffered a heart attack. The patient was on life support. The chances for full recovery looked bleak. The London *Times* had a headline in bold letters that spanned two full pages: "THE FIVE DAYS THAT SHOOK THE WORLD!"

On those same five days, John and I were on a trip with our cousins in a rented house in the hills of Tuscany. Our experience seemed surreal as the disturbing news began to reach us in this remote, idyllic place. Day 1: the Ligurian coast; Day 2: the leaning tower of Pisa; Day 3: the walled city of Lucca; Day 4: eating fried mortadella in a country kitchen at an organic winery; and Day 5: the mountain town of Barga. In spite of the beauty of our surroundings and the novelty of our excursions, the mood of the group was somber and serious, the atmosphere clouded by anxiety, fear, and uncertainty about the future. Surely, each of us anticipated a change in our lifestyles, wondering if the word *depression* would become the reality of our country and the world.

The many things we had counted on for security and stability had proven to be vulnerable. The London *Times* was correct. The world and we were shaken. Things that had seemed permanent and reliable were crumbling around us.

I thought back to our day in Lucca, a city entirely surrounded by a perfectly intact Renaissance wall. Built in the sixteenth century, this formidable bastion was such a deterrent to attack from the neighboring city-states of Florence and Pisa that it was never put to the test. No longer having any military or defensive purpose, the walls now encompass a city park, and a three-mile long avenue of chestnut, plane, and ilex trees. Couples stroll hand in hand, children on bicycles race by, old men sit at tables playing unfathomable Italian card games.

Of the one hundred churches inside the walls of Lucca, only a handful are still active. The rest have been deconsecrated, functioning now as museums or art galleries. The two main features of Lucca: massive walls and churches. Both still intact, but neither serving the purpose for which they were built. The walls are a recreation area, the churches a tourist attraction.

Let's imagine what might have caused this to happen. When the walls were being erected in the sixteenth century, the churches were also being built. As the stones were being put in place to construct the protective wall, as the "tower houses" were built, the people never forgot that their true source of safety and protection was their Lord: their rock, their fortress, their refuge and stronghold. The centuries passed with no enemy invasion. Years of peace led to prosperity because craftsmen and tradesmen could pursue their talents in something other than defense. Curiously, after centuries of peace and security, the people stopped attending their churches, having wandered from their faith. Worship of an invisible rock, fortress, and strong tower seemed almost unnecessary with the walls of Lucca so visible and tangible, something they could see and touch every day. It was easy to believe that the impressive walls had assured their security. Why did they need to put their trust in anything else?

Imagine that finally the enemy invasion did come and the walls came tumbling down. What had seemed so permanent and solid was destroyed. What had seemed indestructible lay in ruins. The walls they had trusted for protection had been vulnerable after all. Something began to change in Lucca. Amid the rubble and devastation of the breached walls, the people cried out to God and returned to their churches. An awakening of faith had begun.

What walls have we built to create a sense of security? Brick by brick—bank accounts, stock portfolios, retirement accounts. Brick by brick—education, social prominence, career. Brick by brick —wealth and possessions. Our walls had been breached by this global financial collapse and we felt assaulted, thrown down, like a leaning wall and a tottering fence (Ps. 62:3).

Is it time to think of rebuilding with things of enduring and lasting quality—faith, simplicity, humility, and service? The Bible gives us a picture of rebuilding walls through the prophet Nehemiah, who rebuilt the walls of Jerusalem after the Babylonian exile. What did Nehemiah do when he learned that the walls of Jerusalem had been broken down and the gates burned with fire? He wept, he praised God, and he confessed. Is this a pattern we should follow?

We probably did our share of weeping and mourning that October in 2008 as the world's economies collapsed and we faced an uncertain future. God wants his children to cry out to him.

In the midst of crisis and uncertainty, can we still praise him? Praise him as our rock, our fortress, our shield, our strength and refuge. When the things we have counted on have been shaken, we can praise him as the one who abides, who never changes. In him we can trust that we are part of something that is "ancient, endless, unstoppable, and unfathomable."[11]

And finally, we need to confess: we, too, can be like the ancient people of God. In times of prosperity and peace when we have eaten and are satisfied (Deut. 6:11), we often forget

God. In pride and self-sufficiency we fall away, our hearts focused on earthly treasures, on the things that "moths and vermin destroy, and . . . thieves break in and steal" (Mt. 6:19). As our riches increase, we set our hearts on them. Do we have to be "in a dry and parched land where there is no water" (Ps. 63:1) before we will seek God earnestly?

When our pride and confidence are shaken, it is time to rediscover humility. The twin pillars of humility have been described as a "[realization of] our own lowliness and God's greatness."[12] Humility helps us acknowledge that God is the source of our only true richness and abundance. We want to know we possess the "riches of his glorious inheritance" (Eph. 1:18); we want to plumb "the depth of the riches of the wisdom and knowledge of God" (Rom. 11:33); we want to grasp the richness of his love, the incomparable riches of the grace that he has lavished on us. Our abundance comes with the acceptance that we are blessed, chosen, redeemed, forgiven, and adopted. We know that if the walls come tumbling down, as they will, we can say with confidence "Truly he is my rock and my salvation; he is my fortress, I will never be shaken" (Ps. 62:2).

PRAYER

L ord, when will we ever learn that you alone are worthy of our trust, the only reliable object of our confidence and hope? How it must grieve your heart when we put our trust in the things we have made with our hands. We mistakenly trust these things because we can see them, touch them, and control them. But, once again, these things will prove to be fallible and vulnerable and as they collapse around us, we cry out in our distress. And, again, we will seek you. And, again, we will know that our God of mercy has never abandoned us. In our disappointment, you will develop our patience, and in dangerous times, you will supply us with your courage. Truly, you are the rock and foundation of our lives; therefore, we will not be shaken.

EIGHT

THE LAND OF COUNTERPANE

I have come that they may have life, and have it to the full.
—John 10:10

*Be on your guard . . . life does not consist in the
abundance of possessions.*
—Luke 12:15

Our Western culture defines richness in terms of health, wealth, education, career, and social status. In the absence of these things, can someone have a life of abundance? A friend named David taught me that it is possible.

As a teenager, David loved working on a ranch and had a special talent with horses. He enjoyed the physical challenge of rodeo riding and became a state champion. A car accident in college left David with spinal cord injuries that caused his life to become more limited over the years. As his mobility deteriorated, he had to give up his specially equipped car, which meant giving up his job. Confined to his home, he still had some independence and enjoyed the companionship of several devoted dogs. Because his condition continued to worsen, he spent his final years in a nursing home. David died at the age of fifty-nine. As a Medicaid patient, bedridden and with only partial use of one arm, he died "poor in the eyes of the world" (Jas. 2:5).

However, at his funeral service I realized that David had died rich in the eyes of God. Friends, family members, and health-care workers spoke about the impact that David's kindness, patience, civility, and optimism had made on their lives. The word *abundance* kept coming to my mind. How could his life that was so lacking in comfort, experience, and opportunity have been abundant?

Returning home after the funeral, I read a poem from *A Child's Garden of Verses* by Robert Louis Stevenson. "The Land of Counterpane" is about a little boy confined to his bed by illness, who keeps himself "happy all the day" with his toy soldiers and ships. David spent years in the Land of Counterpane. Like the little boy, he had learned to be content in circumstances he had not chosen.

The first epistle of Peter refers to those who "would love life and see good days"(1 Pet. 3:10). Isn't this what we all want? To love life and have good days? Peter goes on to wonder if harm will come to those who are followers of good. But harm comes to good people. What do we do when this desire for good days encounters suffering? The answer lies in knowing the reasons for our hope, a hope that is not wishful thinking but something grounded in our faith, a hope that cannot be shaken (not permanently) by tragedy or circumstance.

To David's friends, it seemed that he was experiencing bad days. With diminished health and financial resources, he had no earthly treasures upon which to set his heart. I wonder if this helped him focus on heavenly treasures—the richness of his spiritual blessings, the assurance that grace is sufficient. George MacDonald writes in *Diary of an Old Soul*:

> Lord, loosen in me the hold of visible things;
> Help me to walk by faith and not by sight;
> I would, through thickest veils and coverings,
> See into the chambers of the living light.

Through the veil of illness and disability David had learned to focus on the living light. Do we only learn that Christ is all we need when Christ is all we have? David had discovered a place of abundance in a hospital bed in a run-down nursing home. The foundation of David's hope—faith, family, and friends—created the abundance of his life. Perhaps we need to re-evaluate the components of a good and abundant life and loosen our grasp and affection on the things that "moth and vermin destroy, and . . . thieves break in and steal" (Mt. 6:19).

From David, I learned the value of simplicity. On the outside stairs of the school I attended as a child, a saying was written in stone: "Teach us to delight in simple things." As a wise third-grader, I thought this was a stupid motto, especially for a school where we were learning complicated things! The limitations of his life taught David to appreciate simplicity. The little boy in Stevenson's poem enjoyed the pleasures close at hand on his bedcovers (or counterpane, the old-fashioned term)—ships and toy soldiers, houses, and trees. David's pleasures were also those close at hand, within reach of his one good arm—the TV remote control, a cell phone, a wooden back scratcher, a cigar, Kit Kat candy bars, chewing gum, a warm Pepsi—and a worn Bible. In the midst of the material abundance of our lives—homes, travel, career, sports, and hobbies—might we do well to refine our understanding of abundance by learning to delight in simple things?

From David I learned that suffering or pain should not preclude good manners and kindness. How can you say that a paralyzed man always put his best foot forward? But David did. Every time I visited the depressing nursing home, I was greeted with a smile. His nurses and his room-mate all remarked that he made their day a little brighter.

David's attitude reminded me to find pleasure in the ordinary. He enjoyed watching a football game with a friend, he loved his new refrigerator that turned that warm Pepsi into a more refreshing drink, he loved a choc-olate milkshake and the loan of the DVD series *War and Remembrance*. In the midst of our own abundance of experience and opportunity, have we lost the ability to find pleasure in the ordinary? "There are burning bushes all around. . . . Every tree is full of angels." Will we open our eyes to see that

"Glory comes streaming from the table of daily life," or will we "remain blind to the holy" in our midst?[13]

Because of David, I am going to prepare myself to see the "holy in the ordinary,"[14] to be nourished by the simple gifts at my fingertips, thankful for my daily blessings—for my dog Spencer's brown eyes, the first song of the mourning dove, the smell of my neighbor's piñon logs, the first blade of green sprouting from the hyacinth bulb, the first whiff of a laurel blossom in the spring.

Because of David, I will remember how appealing it is to be around an optimistic person. He was always hopeful that things were going to get better, that he would walk again, that he would be able to live independently, that he would be reunited with his dogs. And, in the meantime, though everyone else knew these things were not going to happen, he did not complain.

Because of David, I want to find the grace to be present in each moment. His razor-sharp memory recalled details and conversations I had forgotten from our teenage years. I had excuses for my bad memory. I reasoned that he remembered the past because that is all he had. His life had stopped while mine had gone on to include husband and children, travels, and so many activities. My memory bank was so full, how could I attend to each one, cherish each one, and remember each one? But David could. Not because his active life had ceased, but because he had always been paying attention to the moments of his life. He had always possessed the gift to find grace in the present moment.

We live in the land of too much or not enough. Had David learned the value of "just enough"? We are often like the ancient Israelites who were not satisfied with God's abundant provision of good things. In spite of daily manna, they craved other food, wailing and complaining for something different. God understood their hearts—and ours. "Would they have enough if flocks and herds were slaughtered for them? Would they have enough if all the fish in the sea were caught for them?" (Num. 11:22). Bob Perks understands that the abundant life derives from appreciating the gift of just enough:

I wish you enough sun to keep your attitude bright.
I wish you enough rain to appreciate the sun more.
I wish you enough happiness to keep your spirit
  alive.
I wish you enough pain so that the smallest joys in
  life appear much bigger.
I wish you enough gain to satisfy your wanting.
I wish you enough loss to appreciate all that you
  possess.[15]

Thank you, David, that although you were "sick and lay abed, with two pillows at your head, the giant great and still that sits upon the pillow hill," you found a way to abundance and pleasure in the Land of Counterpane. You have reminded me of the value of simplicity, the wisdom of being attentive to each moment of the day, the benefit of cherishing the blessings of the ordinary, the appeal of optimism. From you I have learned the true meaning of the abundant life that Jesus promised his followers.

PRAYER

Father, most of us anticipate that we will encounter our own Land of Counterpane, our lives limited in some form. It could be physical disability or illness, like David's, but it could come another way. It could be the paralysis of grief, the burden of responsibility, or the limitation of finances or lack of purpose. Help us to deal with these limitations by remembering to be grateful for blessings that are close at hand. Help us to remember to define our abundance by our faith, family, and friends.

NINE

LOST THINGS

The Son of Man came to seek and save the lost.

—Luke 19:10

I shall lose none of all those he has given me.

—John 6:39

God's character is revealed in many ways—through his Word, through prayer and worship, through other people, and through nature. Living in a house with a pet-to-human ratio of two to one (at least), I have learned much about God through my furry and feathered housemates—dogs, cats, rabbits, and birds.

When we were studying Genesis, I presented Spencer, our Cavalier King Charles Spaniel, as an illustration of sinful and disobedient human nature. Like Adam and Eve in the garden, Spencer had been provided with everything he needed or desired. Still, he disobeyed the one rule of the house: DO NOT chew on my mother's needlepoint rug! Spencer, the sinning spaniel, had fallen from grace. It is time to redeem his reputation.

Four scenes from Spencer's life with tennis balls will illustrate God's unconditional love for the lost:

Scene 1: In our home in North Carolina. Spencer sits by the backyard fence looking forlornly down the mountain where I have thrown an errant tennis ball. John says my problem is that I "throw like a girl." Oh well. With a sad but hopeful heart, Spencer waits in expectation for his precious ball to come back to him. Were it not for the fence, which prevents him from leaving the yard, he would be running down the mountain in active pursuit. We try to distract him. We tempt him with a Greenie, suggest a ride in the VW convertible. He won't leave his post. We offer another ball as a replacement. He is not comforted. He does not forget. He wants only *that* ball, the lost one.

Scene 2: The girl throws another errant ball—this time into the swimming pool. Spencer paces back and forth, whining and distressed. He dips his paw in the water trying to create a current that will draw the ball back within his reach. Sometimes the ball comes close to the edge, but a mountain breeze blows it back to the center of the pool. An irretrievable ball. An inconsolable dog. Spencer continues his frantic vigil. A fresh, dry ball? A ride in the car? A Greenie? There is no substitute or replacement for the drowning ball.

Scene 3: Spencer's head is under the couch, his black bottom is in the air, tail wagging. Although he has been away from this mountain house for eleven months, he remembers there is a tennis ball under the couch. As he lifts the skirt of the couch, light penetrates the darkness and the forgotten, dust-covered ball can be recovered. He is ecstatic.

Scene 4: At our house in San Antonio. A tennis ball has been accidentally thrown into the middle of a rose bush. I caution Spencer, "Don't save that ball—you could get hurt." Spencer is willing to risk the pain of a bloody nose to extract a ball from the tangle of thorns. With a yelp, he emerges triumphant with the ball in his mouth.

If Spencer wore a T-shirt, it would say, "Tennis balls are life." They are his prized possession, his passion, his pleasure, and his preoccupation. Sitting proudly by a basket of new balls from Walmart, he must feel his cup runneth over; he believes he has died and gone to heaven. A gift—undeserved like grace—of clean, bright balls, full of bounce.

In the same way, God loves the righteous—those with

"clean hands" and a "pure heart" (Ps. 24:4). But in the amazing grace of God's unconditional love, he loves us when we are like the old tennis balls that Spencer also cherishes—those that are dirty, damaged, faded, worn, and torn. Those with no bounce left in them.

Has life ever hurled you down the mountain, causing you to tumble from the heights to the lowest valley? Behold your God. He is watching. He will not leave his post as he waits for you to return. There is no valley so deep that he will not find you. God sees your suffering and he hears your cries. Nothing distracts him from his attentive and active concern for your welfare.

Do you sometimes feel as if you are drowning? Under a burden of responsibility, obligation, and duty? Trying to please everyone, fix everything, make everyone happy? Are you drowning under a weight of grief, regret, or disappointment, feeling that you can barely catch your breath or come up for air? Just as you are about to reach the edge of the pool where there is safety, another breeze of circumstance blows you back into the deep end. Behold your God. His hand is always creating a current to draw you close to him, to bring you again to a safe place where your head is above water. "He reached down from on high, and took hold of me; he drew me out of deep waters" (Ps. 18:16).

Do you ever feel neglected or forgotten, as though you are gathering dust in a dark place of your life, powerless to move forward? Do you need someone to remember you, to look for you, to help you come back into the light so you can recover a sense of purpose, of meaning, of significance? Behold your God. He has never forgotten; he knows where you are. He will light your lamp and light up your darkness.

Have you become entangled by the thorns Jesus describes in the parable of the sower? Trapped by the cares and worries of this world, the deceitfulness of wealth? Jesus knew the risk and the pain involved in your rescue. Don't go, Jesus. You could get hurt! Behold your God. He did go. And he was hurt. He wore a crown of thorns to rescue us from the thorns of the world.

Behold God's love for the lost. In *The One and Only*,

Beth Moore writes that "the most mind boggling doctrine of the Word of God is that the Creator and Sustainer of the Universe who dwells in unapproachable light pursues us. He rides the clouds like a chariot and chases after you—his is a love that will not let you go." Our new name is "Sought After." We are sought after by the King of Kings, the Lord of Lords! And when he finds us? Finders, keepers! It sounds like "Find her, keep her."

PRAYER

"Amazing grace, how sweet the sound that saved a wretch like me. I once was lost but now am found . . . ." Most likely, at some point in our lives we have felt like Spencer's lost tennis balls: flung down the mountain, drowning in the pool, languishing and forgotten in a dark place, or entangled in the thorns of the world. Unlike that basket of fresh yellow balls, we can feel dirty, torn, worn down, scarred by life, with no bounce left in us. Behold our God. He watches, he waits, he seeks, and he searches. He and Spencer have a long memory for lost things. They do not forget. They are dedicated and persistent. They will not be distracted or consoled until they are reunited with the lost things. "Where are you?"— the first question of Scripture and a question that is still on the lips of God. "Where are you?"

TEN

SNAPSHOTS OF THE SAVIOR FROM THE BACK PORCHES OF RIDGE RUN ROAD

Lord, you alone are my portion and my cup; you make my lot secure.
The boundary lines have fallen for me in pleasant places.

—Psalm 16:5–6

Photo albums chronicle the significant times in our lives: a newborn baby swaddled in pink or blue, a seven-year-old missing a front tooth, a high school senior in cap and gown. Pictures of friends and family, weddings and vacations.

Among my numerous photo albums is one devoted to pictures taken at our summer home in the Blue Ridge Mountains. All the significant phases of my life have taken place on Ridge Run Road. When I was five years old, my parents rented a house up the street. My brothers and I slid down the mountainside in cardboard boxes on the few days it didn't rain. We worried about passing the swimming test at the nearby lake. We blew dandelions on the way to the inn for bingo night. Chatham blankets from a nearby textile mill were the prizes. Years later, I returned as a college student for a weekend party. My inattentive date played thirty-six holes of golf in one day. A decade later, I returned as a young mother with our ten-month-old son, who has now spent thirty-three summers at this mountain retreat.

In the summer, we walk our dogs on Ridge Run Road or drive in our orange VW convertible, admiring the style of houses, distinctive to this small community: shingles of chestnut bark, brightly painted front doors and shutters, cheerful window boxes, flower gardens, lawn swings, and purple martin birdhouses.

When we were in North Carolina one October, the summer cottages were vacant, everyone having gone down the mountain for the fall and winter months, which gave me an opportunity to admire the familiar houses from a different vantage point. With my camera, I walked up the ridge through the backyards of my neighbors, taking photographs from each back porch. I was struck by the uniqueness of the view from each house. Each view is created by several factors: how the house is positioned on the lot, how high or low it is on the ridge, where the boundary lines were drawn, and whether trees obscure the view. Some back porches have a mountain view, while others see only the valley.

Changing the lenses on my camera helped me focus on different aspects of the view. With the telephoto lens, I was able to identify that little red spot on a distant ridge—a dilapidated barn. The wide-angle lens captured the sweeping panorama from Fisher's Peak in Virginia to Pilot Mountain near Winston-Salem. With a close-up lens, I photographed a ladybug on a rhododendron leaf and a fat, fuzzy bumblebee on a pink geranium.

In a similar way, we are each creating an album that chronicles our life with God. Our snapshots of the Savior remind us of his presence in all the significant phases of our lives. As we continue to photograph God, perhaps we need to experiment with different lenses so that our image of him is broader, more detailed, and more focused.

With a telephoto lens, something distant seems closer—like the red barn I could not distinguish with the naked eye. Why would we need such a lens for a God who is not far from any one of us? "For in him we live and move and have our being" (Acts 17:27–28). Although God is always as near as the air we breathe, in times of doubt or despair we might feel that he has "hidden his face" (Ps. 22:24). This is when we need the telephoto lens of prayer and devotion to bring him back into focus and to remind us that he is never distant. Just past our house, Ridge Run Road veers to the left and goes steeply downhill, the name changing to Devotion Road. Not many people take the challenge of walking down this road because of the steep return climb. If God ever seems distant to you, it is important that you spend some time on devotion road every day.

Just as a wide-angle lens is necessary to photograph the view from Virginia to Winston-Salem, we need a special lens to capture the width, breadth, depth, and length of the nature of God. The wide-angle lens of our faith is memory. The responsibilities and worries of today can keep us from reflecting on our history with God. HIS-STORY as part of our story, his love and grace intersecting our story. Throughout Scripture, God repeatedly tells his people to remember.

A close-up lens magnifies the details of something that is near. It can reveal that a bluebonnet has some red petals, or that a lantana is shaped like a perfect bridal bouquet. We magnify the details of God with gratitude and thanksgiving. We magnify him when we approach his Word with a "slow and steady reverence."[16] Spend a week meditating on one of the attributes of God—his love, faithfulness, goodness, power, or holiness. Absorb the significance of one of the names of Jesus—Shepherd, Physician, Light, Bread, and Living Water. Memorize Scripture. Meditate. Keep a journal. As I meditated on "How lovely is your dwelling place" (Ps. 84:1), I thought about my eternal dwelling and more carefully observed the beauty of the natural world, which was Jesus' dwelling place. I wondered how often I am a lovely dwelling place for God. I paid more attention to the people I encounter every day—they are also God's dwelling place. These are details that are not noticed without the close-up lens of meditation, journaling, and prayer.

So far, we have only composed our photos, enhancing the view with the use of different lenses. We still don't have a print to frame and put on the piano in the living room, a snapshot for our wallet, something to add to the album.

What is the next step? Before the digital age film had to be processed or developed in a darkroom, the photographer usually working in solitude. The key component was the negative, exposed to a special light. Submerging a blank piece of paper into a chemical vat, one waited with expectation, hope, and curiosity for the image to appear. The image began as hazy, but in moments it was a focused and clear picture.

We are continually developing and processing our image of God as we grow in knowledge of him. Like the photographer, we need darkroom times of silence and solitude. We need to offer God the blank spaces of prayer, study, and meditation so his image can become imprinted in our souls and "traces of God become visible."[17] To bring him into focus, we must bring into the darkroom our mountain and valley views. There is no photograph without the negative. The spiritual life is about making "prints out of your own negatives."[18]

Just as each back porch on Ridge Run Road has a unique view of the landscape, so the view of God is probably different on each back porch. Our snapshot of God is determined by our lot in life, whether we are high or low on the road of circumstance, whether something obscures the view, whether we are in the midst of a mountain top experience or walking in the valley of shadows. The people who sit on the back porches of every community have different dreams, hopes, fears, and challenges that shape their image of God. One may need a picture of him as faithful husband, another as Father or friend. One may need to picture him as the great physician, another as daily bread, or light. And, when tragedy comes, the goal may simply be to keep God in focus.

We take comfort from the knowledge that God is the "same yesterday and today and forever" (Heb. 13:8), consistent and never changing. God wants us to grasp the big picture of him: "the God who made the world and everything in it . . . the Lord of heaven and earth" (Acts 17:24). But he will reveal himself according to the particular circumstances on our own back porch, giving us each a wallet-sized photo of himself to carry with us every-place we go—to meet us in our daily need.

PRAYER

We may not like what is happening on our back porch right now. But we must come to terms with the sovereignty of God and find peace within the boundaries that define our life. Help us, Lord, to see you present on our back porch; help us to find peace there. Help us to experience your nearness within those boundaries and to find in them the reason to seek you.

ELEVEN

THE GOOD BOOK

All Scripture is God-breathed and is useful for teaching, rebuking, correcting, and training in righteousness.
—2 Timothy 3:16

Your word is a lamp for my feet, a light on my path.
—Psalm 119:105

My women's book club read and discussed a novel, *A Gate at the Stairs* by Lorrie Moore. In our opinion, it would have been better as a collection of short stories because there were so many tangents and side stories. There was, however, a common theme—the "coming of age" of a college student as she matured through the experiences of change, loneliness, and loss.

The common theme in the three short stories of *this* chapter is the importance of God's Word in our lives as we mature in our faith. Because the future will involve changes of plot and scene, side stories, unpredictable characters, and new chapters, we must be encouraged to:

> ✶ Continue our individual and personal story with the Good Book.
> ✶ Belong to a group with whom to share our journey in God's Word.
> ✶ Approach Scripture as a way to know God, who is the author of these words.

My own journey with the Good Book began when I was given my first Bible at the age of twelve at my Confirmation. The New Testament and Psalms in the King James Version— beige leather, the size of a deck of cards, my name written in turquoise ink on thin onionskin paper. It has a zipper with a cross on the end. On the front page is a picture of Christ knocking at a closed door, his head inclined as if listening for the sound of approaching footsteps. "Here I am! I stand at the door and knock" (Rev. 3:20). He knocked and listened and waited for years. Sometimes I peered with curiosity through a peephole. I occasionally opened the door a crack, but kept the safety chain on to prevent his entry, as if he were the Fuller Brush Man or the Avon Lady selling things I didn't want or didn't think I needed. The little Bible with the zipper was forgotten as it languished on a shelf collecting dust.

In my twenties, I was trying to make sense of several threads and tangents, trying to find a common theme for my life, frequently re-inventing myself. This was in the 1970s, a time of seeking and self-discovery for my generation who came of age in the turbulent 1960s. Who was I? Hippie or debutante? Social worker or legal assistant? Wildlife photographer or aspiring cook studying at Cordon Bleu in Paris, where I nearly cut off my finger while decapitating a duck? With the benefit of hindsight, I see that there was a thread weaving together all these contradictory aspects of my life—the love of God for his wandering, lost, confused, and reluctant child—a love that was drawing me ever closer to him, even though I was unaware.

At a low point in this period of my life, a package arrived from my cousin in Atlanta. A Bible—hardcover, pale blue, "Holy Bible" in silver. An odd gesture since neither of us was a Christian at the time. I loved it; I cherished it; I looked at it and I touched it. But I didn't open it or read it. At some level, though, I knew it would be valuable and important for my life *one day*. Just having it in my possession gave me some comfort. Finally, I did open the door to the patient Christ and also opened that blue book. There I discovered the power of words to change a life.

The second story illustrates the impact that words have when shared, studied, and discussed within the fellowship of a group. *The Guernsey Literary and Potato Peel Pie Society*, a best-selling novel by Mary Ann Shaffer and Annie Barrows, shows the importance of good books (not the Good Book) on the small community of Guernsey, one of the Channel Islands just off the coast of France, during World War II. Since these undefended islands were a part of Great Britain, they were invaded by the Germans in 1940 and then occupied for the remaining five years of the war. Life for these isolated British islanders was bleak. Their children had been evacuated to England for safety before the Germans arrived. Food was scarce and most of the trees were chopped down for firewood. Outside news or letters were not allowed.

A group of ordinary townspeople formed the literary society (hence the novel's title), which enhanced the lives of its members as they gathered to read and discuss good books. They discovered joy in reading. The relationships created around books helped dispel their isolation and loneliness as they became dearer to one another, strangers becoming friends, almost like family. The group brought out the best qualities of its members and helped them momentarily forget the darkness outside. One member of the society, Eben Ramsey, drew inspiration from a sentence in his favorite book, *Selections from Shakespeare*: "The bright day is done and we are for the dark." If he'd known those words when the Germans landed, "I'd have been consoled somehow and ready to go out and contend with circumstance—instead of my heart sinking to my shoes."[19] The power of good books for this group of friends on Guernsey is similar to the power the Good Book has on our own lives. Especially as we interact with it in a group, it sustains, uplifts, fortifies, instills courage, and keeps hope alive.

My third story reminds us of the reason we read the Good Book—to know God as he is revealed through his Word. If we try to know God apart from his Word, we might be creating a picture of him that is incomplete or inaccurate. I did that as a child. Unfamiliar with the Bible,

I simply invented the God I wanted, imagining him to be like my paternal grandfather, who died when I was five—a kind and gentle white-haired gentleman (he was born in 1875!) who lived far away and visited only occasionally. A sweet man who winked at my misbehavior, patted me on the head, and said, "Be a good girl." This picture of him remained inaccurate and incomplete until years later when I got to know him through his own words.

When my grandfather graduated from medical school, he moved to the Oklahoma Territory (before it was a state) and began his career as a horse-and-buggy doctor. Later, he was the dean of the University of Oklahoma Medical School, regarded as an international authority on tuberculosis. After my grandmother's death in 1978, a box was found in her attic—full of my grandfather's personal diaries. I asked if I could have them. At the time, our son Jeff was a baby whose daily naptimes gave me the opportunity to read the diaries, which I edited into a book published for the members of my family.

The entries in the diaries, which spanned thirty years, covered an astonishing range of subjects from medical notes, reminders, and professional observations to evocative reflections on all aspects of life. Immersing myself in my grandfather's words, I felt that I knew his heart, character, and passions. He loved to be outdoors fishing and camping, especially when accompanied by his youngest child and only son, my father. He was devoted to his family and his medical practice. An avid reader of all kinds of literature and poetry, he always had a stack of books by the bedside. He was also a successful writer, with two published books, *Pioneer Doctor* and *Tuberculosis and Genius*, both reviewed in *Time* magazine.

My grandfather had become real to me as I read his diaries. Through his words, he had become a mentor, an example and an inspiration for me to live a good life. Had I inherited his character and qualities? Am I like him? Do I resemble him in appearance? Would my life please him and make him proud?

As the child increasingly knows the heart of the Father

through God's Word, he will begin to "hunger after the life of which he is capable,"[20] and the Word will be "conceived and clothed in flesh and lived out in our lives," no longer merely "written and silent, only to pass away."[21] It is only as we know God that we can begin to live, act, and love as he does, which is the goal of our faith journey. After all, we are children who have inherited the attributes and qualities of the Father. And we should wonder. Are we like him? Do our lives look like his? Are we pleasing him?

An entry in my grandfather's diary helped me to understand the motivation for us to "come of age" and mature as Christians who more and more resemble the Father. On February 14, 1937, after spending a weekend in New York with his son (my father), then a freshman at Dartmouth College, my grandfather wrote in his diary:

> What a day. I do not even know whether the sun was shining. The light was with me and in me— my boy fine and well. I saw him, lived with him, ate and slept with him, touched and loved him. We communed intellectually and spiritually as of old— sitting arm and arm through the wonderful experience of seeing Helen Hayes in *Regina*. I put him on the train and said goodbye. How rich we are in beautiful children.

In a letter written after their weekend together, my father expressed his gratitude:

> Dad, you can't know how much it meant to see you last weekend. Your letter written Sunday from NY was the sweetest thing in the world. I'll keep it always among the dearest things I have. I think you are the best father any boy ever had. I'm so glad we have so much in common and we've had so many wonderful things to remember. I'll never forget them. They have done me more good than all the college education in the world. If I don't make a success out of life, it won't be your fault.

No one could have been a better father than you've been. I love you, Dad, and want you to be proud of me so much. Your best pal and son, Lewis.

Grateful for his father's love, this young man's response was a desire to live a life worthy and pleasing. When we understand God's Word as his love letter to us, his children, then we have found our motivation to live a life worthy and pleasing of our Father. The love of our heavenly Father has been lavished upon us. Simply, we respond. "Mercy understood is holiness desired."[22]

We each have a story of our individual involvement with God's Word: the verses we have highlighted and underlined in our Bibles, the notes written in the margin that chronicle our growth as we have matured through grief, loss, success, and failure. We each have cherished memories of Bible studies we have done, leaders whom we have admired, and teachers who have inspired us. But most important, we have grown in our knowledge of the Author of these words. And we know the power of the Word to strengthen, comfort, challenge, and transform us as we come of age in our journey. Grateful for your love, we respond.

TWELVE

THE LADYBUG CASTS
A LONG SHADOW

Do not merely listen to the word . . . . Do what it says.
—James 1:22

*What good is it, my brothers and sisters, if someone claims
to have faith but has no deeds?*
—James 2:14

*The fruit of the Spirit is love, joy, peace, forbearance, kindness, goodness,
faithfulness, gentleness and self-control.*
—Galations 5:22–23

Anna Quindlen's novel *Every Last One* is about an ordinary family whose lives are shattered by an unthinkable act of violence. The theme centers on the consequences that stem from actions that appear to be inconsequential. A quote from the novel lingered in my mind. The mother sits in the backyard enjoying the evening breeze when the child wonders if "the beating of [butterfly] wings in Mexico could cause a breeze in [her] backyard."[23] The butterfly effect. Although Quindlen explores the far-reaching consequences of an evil act, the same idea can be seen in a positive light. Deeds of kindness that we deem insignificant and unremarkable can reverberate and ripple into the future.[24]

My ruminations on this idea were given a visual

component one October when we were inundated with ladybugs in the Blue Ridge Mountains. They were in the house, on your clothes, and in the fur of the dog. Because I could not ignore them, I Googled "swarms of ladybugs" to see if their numbers forecast an impending weather system or were simply the result of a rainy autumn.

Sitting on the porch one afternoon, something caught my eye. With the sun shining on one of these tiny, spotted oval-shaped domes, the ladybug cast a shadow nearly ten times its size.

"The ladybug casts a long shadow" seemed a potential title for a talk for my Bible-study group. The sunlight created the elongated shadow of the ladybug. In a similar way, if we live in the light of the Son, the deeds we consider insignificant and unremarkable might cast a shadow of blessing into the future. We are blessed to be a blessing. If we are to be a blessing in the life of another person, is it the result of faith alone? Is it enough just to have faith that Jesus is Lord and Savior and to trust in unmerited grace? Or is a blessing paid forward only as we become *doers* of the Word, by living out the good works that God has prepared in advance for us to do (Eph. 2:10)?

Christians have a "complex relationship with the idea of work."[25] A new believer gratefully embraces the truth that he is "justified by faith alone, apart from the works of the law," but he or she might be confused to hear James' exhortation that faith without works is "barren," "worthless," and "dead." "Holding these two claims together can be a tough balancing act."[26] We err on the side of legalism if we focus too much on works. But we risk being called lazy and unfruitful if we have too little focus on works.

We just can't get away from the fact that in order to bless others, Christians must do something. If the evidence of our faith is works, what does this look like in our lives? When I became a Christian thirty years ago, eager to serve God and others, I worried that *doing* the Word might involve packing up the family and moving to Africa as missionaries. Thankfully, a Christian friend, more mature in her faith, told me simply to "bloom where you are planted."

Two people have helped me to understand the "works" that please God.

Birdie Lasater was an OLD friend, who had known five generations of my family. She died at the age of 102. "Well done, good and faithful servant" was on the program at her funeral service. What had Birdie done in her life? Nothing big, nothing that made the newspapers. She was not a prominent member of the community, with a multi-columned obituary listing numerous boards and civic organizations. What Birdie had done was goodness, kindness, and love. Birdie bloomed where she was planted, for years as a weekly volunteer with Meals on Wheels, serving hot meals to the homebound elderly. She was a greeter in her small Presbyterian church for fifty years and continued greeting people after she moved into the nursing home in her nineties. As one speaker at her funeral commented, she is probably "greeting people in heaven." We would do well to shape our lives around the hymns sung at Birdie's funeral: "My Hope Is Built on Nothing Less," "Near to the Heart of God," and "Jesus Thy Boundless Love to Me."

Birdie made an impact on the character of my children in the many visits we made to her simple home when they were young. Unable to attend her funeral, my son Jeff emailed me: "Thanks for making Birdie a part of our lives." Jeff had worked with a big box of tools that had belonged to Birdie's late husband, Frenchie. We enjoyed many tea parties at her dining room table and many Christmas seasons when Jeff and Millie helped decorate her home. On the shelf above her nursing home bed were seashells my children had given Birdie twenty-six years earlier. When Jeff became an Eagle Scout, Birdie attended the ceremony and shared with him the Silver Beaver Award that had been given to Frenchie as a long-time Scout leader. Birdie knew that God was the basis of her hope and strength; she lived close to the heart of God and knew of his boundless love. A stream of living water flowed from her as she touched many lives. Her gentle character and joyful spirit will be remembered.

The second individual revealed how the simple gift

of hospitality and kindness can create future blessings. A young Marine, sent to fight in the Pacific in WWII, was seriously wounded at Guadalcanal and then spent several months recuperating in a U.S. Navy hospital in Auckland, New Zealand. Although the other soldiers in his hospital ward were sent home to the United States, this was not his fate. In fact, after he recovered he returned to his Marine battalion and fought in the bloody battles of Tarawa, Kwajalein, Saipan, and Tinian. One Sunday during his convalescence in New Zealand, homesick and lonely, he walked on crutches to St. Andrew's Presbyterian Church in downtown Auckland. A local family, the McDonalds, members of the church, took this young soldier under their wings, invited him to their home, welcomed him into their family, and showed him all around the beautiful North Island of New Zealand.

Sixty years later the former Marine, now an old man in his mid-eighties, spent months sharing his war memories with one of his sons, resulting in the publication of his memoir as a book titled *Only a Khaki Shirt*. After all the years, he clearly remembered the kindness of the McDonalds. The old man decided to make a significant financial donation to St. Andrew's Church in their memory, his only condition that the church would display a plaque honoring the McDonald family "for their kindness and generosity to the Second Division of the U.S. Marine Corps during the Second World War." Since the old man could no longer travel, he asked his twenty-six-year old grandson to make the long trip to New Zealand to dedicate the plaque on New Zealand's Day of Remembrance, an annual commemoration of the many New Zealanders who died in the First and Second World Wars. The grandson stood before a full congregation and honored his grandfather by telling the story of the kindness of the McDonalds, who had long since died without any surviving family in Auckland.

The old man was my father-in-law, Baine Kerr, who died in May 2008. The young man was my son Jeff.

Birdie and the McDonalds were blessed to be a blessing. They were the hands and feet of Christ, heeding the advice of D. L. Moody that "every Bible should be bound in shoe leather." They walked the walk and when they talked the talk, the words they spoke were in alignment with the Word they followed. They bore the fruits of the Christian life because they remained connected to Jesus, the source of the harvest of fruit. Their hearts were the good soil that Jesus spoke of in his parable—hearts that were well tended and prepared so they could receive the Word and bear the fruit of the Spirit: "love, joy, peace, forbearance, kindness, goodness, faithfulness, gentleness, and self-control" (Gal. 5:22–23). Each of these is a work that pleases God.

A few months after I had written this essay, John and I were hiking in the Blue Ridge Mountains, where we encountered a couple who live in North Carolina. They were delighted to find Texans who loved the magnificent view from this ridge. We all agreed how blessed we were to be there. As they walked away, the man turned around and said, "You are already a good memory." And then I realized the thread that connects these stories. Kindness is a good memory, a story that is told and retold.

Thank you, Birdie, for showing me that small acts of kindness and service can have a big impact. Thank you, Mr. and Mrs. McDonald, for reminding us not to grow weary of doing good even though we may never see the results of our actions.

The butterfly effect. The shadow of the ladybug. They exemplify the philosophy of Saint Theresa, "the Saint of the little way"—doing the little things in life well and with great love. Their lives show that the "butterfly effect" that casts a shadow of blessing into the future emanates from bearing the fruit of the Spirit—love, joy, peace, patience, and kindness.

Father, your Word does not suggest that we bear fruit but rather commands it, expects it. Help us remember that apart from an abiding relationship with you, we will not bear the fruit of the Spirit. Only if your Word is implanted in our hearts will it grow into the behavior and action that pleases you. Let us not grow weary or discouraged with doing good when we don't see the result. We may plant a tree whose shade we will never sit under. But we hope to hear the words one day, "Well done, good and faithful servant."

THIRTEEN

THE GIRL AND
THE ELEPHANT

For now we see only a reflection as in a mirror; then we shall see face to face.
Now I know in part; then I shall know fully,
even as I am fully known.

—1 Corinthians 13:12

A photo on a greeting card says something to me about our relationship to God. A little girl sits on a wooden stool next to an elephant, her arm extended as far as it will go as she tries to embrace her pachyderm pal. Although it is impossible for her to wrap her arms all the way around him, she leans contentedly against his vast leathery side, enjoying the small part of him that she can reach. Like the little girl, we would like to wrap our arms (minds and hearts) around the whole truth of God but we cannot. "If a picture paints a thousand words, then why can't I paint you?" might be our song to God. In the Sicilian town of Cefalù, the Byzantine-era church has an enormous mosaic of the face of Christ above the altar. The promise of eternity is that we will have a seat in the first pew where we will see him "face to face," knowing him fully. But while we are in this earthly tent (2 Cor. 5:1) we must be content to know him only in part, as we seek his face through his Word, through prayer, worship, study, and fellowship with other believers. We add a splash of color here and there as we grow in our understanding, but our portrait of God remains incomplete until we are in heaven.

Like a small Limoges box, we are containers with a limited capacity for what we can hold. Our "jars of clay" (2 Cor. 4:7) are limited by our finite understanding, finite knowledge, and finite experience. We contain so much of the world, its worries and enticements, that there is not room enough for us to contain all of God. In one of my Limoges boxes, I keep a tiny cross, a reminder that although God is fully present in all the moments of our lives, we are limited in what we can grasp. Remembering the girl and the elephant, we know we must hold onto what we can understand and know about God, cherishing small insights and revelations. We need to lean contentedly against that part of him that we can embrace.

Jesus understood our limitation to grasp the whole truth of God. "I have much more to say to you, more than you can now bear" (Jn. 16:12). Perhaps Jesus didn't want us to have the experience of Isaiah who saw the King, the Lord of Hosts, and said, "Woe to me; I am ruined" (Isa. 6:5).

By sending Jesus, God was making himself more accessible. The pillar of cloud and fire became flesh and blood and lived among us. Jesus took the great but incomprehensible "I AM" and broke it down into more understandable and manageable terms that we can embrace and wrap our arms around: I am shepherd, I am light, I am bread, I am living water, I am the gate, I am the true vine, I am the way, the truth, and the life.

We are familiar with the Christian classic *Your God Is Too Small* by J. B. Phillips. But we may sometimes feel that our God is too big. Before we are in heaven, finally capable of grasping the fullness of God, we may need to digest and understand him in smaller pieces. Because God wants us to grow in our knowledge, he invites us to a spiritual sip-and-see. Although the Living Water is all the oceans of the world, Niagara Falls and Victoria Falls combined, he offers us a straw so we can take sips. My Limoges box can only hold two tablespoons of water. We cannot contain all the Living Water now, but we can quench our thirst with enough to keep us nourished and refreshed. Scripture says to "taste and see that the Lord is good" (Ps. 34:8). Although the great banquet awaits us in heaven, we are now presented with a tasting menu, daily portions of bite-size manna to assuage our hunger for him. Sip by sip, bite by bite, we internalize him in portions we can assimilate.

But to me somehow it feels wrong to compartmental- ize God, dividing him into smaller portions to suit my age or stage of life, accommodating him to my limitations. As I struggle with this dilemma, I read from Saint Augustine in his *Confessions* and realize he felt the same. Awe at the vastness of God, while recognizing his limited capacity to grasp his magnitude: "O Thou, the greatest and the best, mightiest, almighty, most merciful and most just, utterly hidden and utterly present, most beautiful and most strong, abiding yet mysterious, suffering no change and changing all things, ever in action, ever at rest, gathering all things to Thee." I agree with you, Augustine, our God is so big. Augustine continues:

> What room is there in me for the God who made heaven and earth. Is there anything in me, O God, that can contain You. Are you not in every place at once in the totality of Your being, while yet noth- ing contains you wholly? The house of my soul is too small to receive thee. Does this mean that we only contain part of You?

But we are impatient to sit on the front pew to behold the face of God, ready to complete our portrait of him, eager to embrace the fullness of the great I AM, thirsty for all the Living Water in a Big Gulp, hungry for the whole loaf of bread at the great banquet. We want to be like Isaiah who saw the "Lord, high and exalted, seated on a throne" (Isa. 6:1). The greeting card photograph of the girl and the elephant helps me to be patient and content with what I can understand about God today. No, she cannot embrace the whole elephant. God may be saying to us:

- ⁎ Embrace me as your hope when you despair.
- ⁎ Embrace me as your counselor when you are confused.
- ⁎ Embrace me as the Prince of Peace when you are anxious.
- ⁎ Embrace me as your resting place when you are weary.
- ⁎ Embrace me as your joy when you are downhearted.
- ⁎ Embrace me as the Way when you are lost.
- ⁎ Embrace me as your friend when you are lonely.
- ⁎ Embrace me as your strength when you are weak.
- ⁎ Embrace me as your Savior when you have sinned.

PRAYER

Father, we cherish the gift and the blessing that we shall know you fully and see you in your Glory. We yearn for the full revelation that awaits us in eternity when we are finally empty of the world and able to contain you wholly. In the meantime, we will be content to sip and taste, because you would rather we embrace the part of you that we can grasp than not seek you at all.

FOURTEEN

WINDBLOWN

*Suddenly a sound like the blowing of a violent wind
came from heaven.*

—Acts 2:2

*The wind blows wherever it pleases. You hear its sound, but you cannot
tell where it comes from or where it is going.*

—John 3:8

When a dear friend, a member of our Bible study group, died of cancer in 2010, we were once again reminded that the topic of suffering is one we cannot avoid. As Christians, we feel we should be prepared and equipped to handle it—and in a different way from nonbelievers. But we worry. How will we cope with it when it comes to us, or comes again? Will our faith stand firm? Will joy, peace, and trust endure? Will we maintain the hope that is "an anchor for the soul" (Heb. 6:19)? Or will we be like "mists driven by a storm" (2 Pet. 2:17) or like a "wave of the sea, blown and tossed by the wind" (Jas. 1:6)? Might suffering make us as fragile as a dandelion scattered on the wind by the breath of a child? One thing is certain: there is no get-out-of-jail-free card to hardship.

Richard Foster, in *Life with God*, writes, "The spiritual life is not climbing a ladder of perfection, but embracing one's wounds and finding the transforming power of God at work in them."[28] When we put on the spectacles of Divine Providence, we acknowledge the truth of this statement. In hindsight, we understand that suffering has indeed transformed us. In enduring, our faith has been tested and the result has been growth and maturity. But, grief can also overwhelm our trust in God and leave us questioning our faith.

The truth is that we would prefer to have wisdom without the wounds, growth without grief, maturity without the misery. We would prefer the easy path. Health, wealth, happiness, perfect children, devoted spouses. When we read that God protects us, we wish it were a forecast for smooth sailing ahead, calm waters, and blue skies. Perhaps we shouldn't wish for such a protected life. George Herbert wrote, "Storms are the triumph of his art." My former pastor said, "Calm seas did not a sailor make." When James wrote "consider it pure joy, my brothers and sisters, whenever you face trials of many kinds" (Jas. 1:2), he understood that God shapes us in the midst of the struggles. But how do we strengthen our sea legs? How do we find the inner strength to face these trials?

The natural world confirms spiritual truths because God's "invisible qualities—his eternal power and divine nature—have been clearly seen" (Rom. 1:20). Three teachers have shown me that suffering can make us resilient, strong, and beautiful: the Joshua tree, the flowers of Cornwall, and a spider who wove his web in the Blue Ridge Mountains.

The Joshua Tree

In Jeannette Walls's memoir *The Glass Castle*, a young girl and her mother are walking where the desert ends and the mountain begins, a virtual wind tunnel. Coming upon the Joshua tree, "scraggly and freakish, permanently stuck in its twisted, tortured position," the child wanted to dig it up and replant it near the house where it would be protected from the wind. The mother disagreed, "You'd be destroying what makes it special. . . . It's the Joshua tree's struggle that gives it its beauty."[29]

The wind of cancer blew into our friend's life and took it. But like the Joshua tree, the wind did not take away her beauty. She was like the "tree planted by streams of water, which yields its fruit in season" (Ps. 1:3). Though the wind blew hard and relentlessly, the fruit of the Spirit remained. Though her body weakened, joy, peace, gentleness, and kindness held strong. And we witnessed beauty in the midst of her struggle.

The Flowers of Cornwall

In May 2009 we spent a week on the north coast of Cornwall with our daughter, who was then living in London. The wind rattled the windows of the gray-shingled cottage, "Pentonwarra," built into the side of a rocky cliff overlooking the blue-green Celtic Sea. We walked for hours on the path that follows the coastline, admiring the dramatic panorama of cliff and ocean, the secluded coves and large sandy beaches created by the force of wind and wave. After a few days, I began to notice the details, literally under my feet—the flowers growing on both sides of the ancient stone wall bordering the path. The wall was covered by thick, spongy moss out of which cheerful pink and yellow flowers grew in abundance. Buffeted by the constant wind, this is a harsh environment for these tiny, delicate flowers. While taking many photographs, I noticed something that surprised me. The flowers growing on the side of the wall that took the full force of the wind were the most beautiful; their colors were vibrant and intense. They grew thick and strong, their roots deep. The flowers on the protected side of the wall were weak, leggy, less vibrant, less intense. They looked as if a gentle breeze might uproot them.

Our daughter was having a difficult time during our Cornwall retreat, facing the fact her job might be in jeopardy because of the economic collapse. Since college, her dream had been to live and work in London. She hated the thought of moving, of starting over, perhaps changing her career. In a shop on Kensington Church Street in London,

I bought her an antique locket into which I placed one of the hardy flowers of Cornwall. With the gift, I wrote a note explaining the lesson of the Joshua tree and the flowers of Cornwall. Don't fear the wind of change and challenge. Put your roots deep into your faith, family, and the promise of God, "I know the plans I have for you . . . to give you hope and a future" (Jer. 29:11). Don't be motivated by a desire for too much safety and protection. Do not retreat too quickly for shelter, but "let the gales sigh through you—to fit you for the winter."[30]

The Industrious Spider of the Blue Ridge

One summer at our house in North Carolina, I sat in the early morning near the porch railing, a space I shared with a tiny spider. Admiring its web as the first rays of the sun made it sparkle a pinkish-gold, I observed its construction. Three anchor lines made of "safety line silk" form an upside-down triangle. Within this anchored triangle, the spider spins its orb web that resembles the spokes of a wheel. One night, a terrific mountain storm roared through the gap, keeping me awake. Admittedly, it is a bit odd to lose sleep worrying about a spider, fearful that its finely embroidered web was being ripped and torn by the force of the wind. The morning revealed that although the center spiral had sustained some damage, the web itself had withstood the storm because the anchor lines had held fast. In a few days, this industrious spider had completely mended its web. Confronted with many storms, it had learned that rebuilding is possible. Giving up in discouragement and accepting defeat was not an option.

To withstand the storms that come our way, we must have our anchor lines secure: the anchor of hope in Christ, "an anchor for the soul, firm and secure" (Heb. 6:19); the anchor of his steadfast love from which we can never be separated; and finally, the anchor of his strength that is "made perfect in weakness" (2 Cor. 12:9).

The Joshua tree, the flowers of Cornwall, and the spider web had all been windblown. The force of wind had shaped the Joshua tree into something beautiful, it had made the Cornwall flowers strong, and it had created resilience in the mountain spider. Is Bob Dylan correct when he sings, "The answer, my friend, is blowin' in the wind"? Only if we look for the answer in the mighty wind of the Holy Spirit, allowing it to sweep through our lives, our heart, our imagination.[31]

God's presence in Scripture is at times represented as wind; the Hebrew word for spirit is *ru'ach*, meaning wind or breath. It is a force that is invisible but whose effects can be seen. It is a wind that blows where it will, a wind we cannot control because we cannot tell where it is coming from or where it is going (Jn. 3:8). It may intersect our lives with the force of a hurricane or it can be as gentle as a whisper. A lovely Irish blessing has the phrase "may the wind be always at your back." God is a following wind that urges us forward when we feel powerless. He is also the wind beneath our wings that uplifts and sustains when we are brought low by suffering. And, he is the surrounding wind that envelops our days. If we have been filled by that wind, we can hang on tight and put our roots down deep, confident that the anchor lines will hold.

PRAYER

Father, we prefer calm seas and gentle breezes. When the strong wind blows, we are fearful and we react like the disciples in the boat with Jesus when the storm raged, saying, "Lord save us, we are going to drown." Then we must remember that you are still the calming power. We sing "Be still my soul . . . the waves and winds still know his voice who ruled them when he dwelt below."[32] When the wind rips apart our carefully constructed plans and hopes, we can rebuild again and again because of "One who makes us brave and strong by being brave and strong beside us."[33]

FIFTEEN

CHARING CROSS

I consider everything a loss because of the surpassing worth of knowing Christ Jesus my Lord.
—Philippians 3:8

For I resolved to know nothing while I was with you except Jesus Christ.
—1 Corinthians 2:2

A few years ago, my family spent Christmas in London because our daughter was living and working there. Therefore, we did minimal decorating at home with a small, artificial tree that we could unplug and move from room to room and, of course, our beautiful Nativity scene. I carefully arranged the figures on the refectory table in the front hall, but apparently someone else (guess who?) had different ideas. It was like playing a game of chess with an invisible person. The angel was moved from the field with the shepherds to a position near the manger. I always place Joseph at the entrance to the stable, standing protectively as the unexpected visitors—shepherds and later, wise men— begin to arrive. Someone else prefers Joseph inside the stable so he can look down adoringly on this mystery child. And so it continued. Angels, sheep, camels, wise men, Mary, and Joseph changed positions daily. But the baby Jesus was never moved. He remained the central figure around whom the others orbited as the planets orbit the sun. The Baby Jesus was their focus, their reference point.

And so the idea of the centrality of Christ was on my mind as we began the trip to London. Christ, central to my life, Christ my main reference point. This trip reminded me that we can have misguided reference points, things we turn to when we are afraid, confused, lost, or hurt. As a fearful flyer, having a senior pilot with a sufficient amount of gray hair calms my anxiety with the assurance that he has survived hundreds of transatlantic flights. Surely, with my assistance, we will both survive this flight as well. When darkness comes to the cabin, I locate a bright star that keeps its fixed and unmoving place outside my small window. If we encounter turbulence, I relax when I look out and see that star.

Once we arrived in London, another misguided reference point helped with my poor sense of direction. Exploring this large city, I needed something large and well known and easy to find, so I could locate our daughter's Knightsbridge flat and our hotel. Harrods was my choice. This huge department store would help me keep my bearings and orientation.

A senior pilot? A star? A store? Wrong reference points. Surely I could do better than this. God is the one with experience and knowledge upon whom I should rely. God is the fixed and steadfast light. God is bigger and better known than Harrods! "Some trust in chariots and some in horses, but we trust in the name of the Lord our God" (Ps. 20:7).

London has its challenges. It can be confusing. At least I understood the language . . . until I encountered the pub menu: bubble-and-squeak, bangers and mash. Chips are crisps and fries are chips. London can be dangerous. Every street crossing has the words "LOOK RIGHT OR LOOK LEFT" so the visitor is not run over by a double-decker red bus. London can make no sense geographically. Charming neighborhoods—Chelsea, Knightsbridge, Notting Hill, Holland Park—seem so distinct and so separate. How are they related to one another? They once were separate villages that became connected as the city grew, in time becoming London.

I became more confident in London when I learned that the city has a recognized geographical center, Charing Cross, located just outside the railway terminal of the same name near Trafalgar Square. All distances into London are measured to this location. Samuel Johnson believed that "the full tide of human existence is at Charing Cross."[34] The cross that stands in front of the railway station is one of the three remaining Eleanor crosses, placed by Edward I to mark the funeral procession of his queen as it made its way to Westminster Cathedral in 1290. It was also the place where the wounded soldiers of World War I and World War II arrived from the battlefront in France, in need of healing, rest, renewal, and reunion.

Charing Cross was also important to a little girl, lost in London. A London bobby tried to help the sobbing child by asking for her address or phone number. In her distress, she couldn't give him any helpful information that would reunite her with her family. When the policeman asked if there was something in her neighborhood that she saw every day, she brightened and replied, "I know the Cross; . . . Show me the cross and I can find my way home. . . ."[35]

Our lives can parallel my experience of London. The world does not always speak our language. We look for the language of kindness, gentleness, and encouragement and find instead the language of condemnation and judgment, of rudeness and vulgarity. With Christ at the center of our hearts, we will hear his language of love, forgiveness, and comfort.

As we look right or look left to avoid the danger of oncoming traffic, so in our lives we try to anticipate from what direction pain and suffering might come our way. As we cross the streets of our life journey, we yearn for clear direction—when to stop, when to yield, when to go, which way to turn. As we navigate, we need to remember that "the

Lord upholds [us] with his hand" (Ps. 37:24), and we will ultimately be crossing to safety.

Our lives can resemble the neighborhoods of London—random and unconnected. We wander through events and circumstances that don't make much sense, wanting to understand the whole picture. Only God has the bird's eye view, the aerial photograph. Trust "that things can come together again, and that again the center can hold."[36]

We can become lost in our spiritual lives like the little girl was lost in London, not knowing how to get home, having lost our landmarks or sense of direction. Like her, we must remember that the cross is the landmark of our neighborhood. If we will see it every day, we will never wander far from home.

And sometimes we are wounded and weary from fighting the good fight (1 Tim. 6:12), bruised from battles with people and circumstances. We need to return home to the center—for rest, renewal, and healing.

Learning that London has a center had made the city more manageable and understandable. And the same holds true for our lives. When we returned home from our trip, the Nativity scene confirmed this as I saw the baby Jesus still at the center—the centrality of Christ. Central to Mary's emotions and ponderings, central to the wise men's seeking, central to Joseph's obedience, central to the shepherds' joy. God wants to be the central focus in the midst of our changing circumstances. But we must make a decision to devote ourselves to this.

So, buy a ticket for the London Tube—the Central Line, of course. Leave the outlying suburbs for the center of the city. Destination: Charing Cross. It will cost you something and the journey takes time. The train makes many stops and you may be tempted to disembark. No matter, just get back on the train. You are headed home, where a person, Christ, waits to welcome you, to embrace the lost and heal the wounded.

Your destination is near.

PRAYER

Our lives will only make sense if we keep you central in them by living near the cross. Help us increasingly to put you in the middle of our choices, our behavior and relationships. We want you central in our celebration and our suffering. We want to hear your language of love and forgiveness, to know you as our guide when we are in unfamiliar places, as the one who is our home when we are lost, the one who heals our wounds.

SIXTEEN

THE HEART OF THE RESCUER

*In your righteousness, rescue me and deliver me; turn your ear
to me and save me. Be my rock of refuge . . .
for you are my rock and my fortress.*

—Psalm 71:2–3

In his hands he gently bears us, rescues us from all our foes.

—Henry F. Lyte

The words *deliver, rescue,* and *save* can be used synonymously. The frequent use of these words in Scripture reveals that rescue may be one of the greatest themes throughout the Bible—the salvation and deliverance of a people, a nation, and of individuals. God as rescuer. What is his nature in this regard? Can we call on him when we're in trouble and trust him to come to our rescue? Do we need to be worthy to merit his saving intervention, or merely recognize that we are sometimes helpless to save ourselves?

Our rescuing God is beautifully portrayed in the Bible as a shepherd. In the Old Testament, he feeds the sheep, strengthens the weak, heals the sick, binds the injured, brings back the strayed, seeks the lost, and rescues those who have been scattered on a day of clouds and thick darkness (Ezek. 34). In the New Testament, Jesus is the good shepherd who knows each sheep by name and protects them, even to the point of laying down his life for them (Jn. 10).

The parable of the lost sheep reveals the mindset and

heart of the shepherd. He was vigilant, watchful, and protective of his flock of one hundred sheep. One evening, as he inspected and counted his sheep at the end of the day, he was surprised and grieved to discover that one was missing. He knew that apart from his protection, this animal was defenseless and in grave danger. The shepherd did not delay; he did not rest but made haste to search for the lost, determined that "no one will snatch them out of my hand" (Jn. 10:28). Why is this one so valuable? If it were merely a financial crisis, surely it would be more prudent to protect the ninety-nine than to leave them while searching for one lost sheep. It can only be explained by how much the shepherd loved the lamb he had raised since its birth. He will persist until the lost one is found. He covered miles, always watching, always listening for a cry of distress. Finally, he heard a faint bleating. He lifted the weary, frightened lamb and put it on his shoulders (Lk. 15:5). And then what did he do? Rather than returning quickly to check on the sheep left behind, he gave us a glimpse of heavenly emotions as he gathered friends and neighbors to join with him in rejoicing over the lost sheep that has been found: "the joy of heaven when the lost one is found."

I like the idea of being a rescuer; on occasion, I have rescued someone's pet that was not in need of my help. "Lady, why are you putting my cat in your car?" But one time an animal really did need saving and I jumped at the opportunity. On a cold, moonlit night at our ranch, John and I were sitting by a fire close to the creek. Steep limestone cliffs rise on the other side of the water. The silence of the starry night was broken by a cry of distress. What could it be? We remembered that earlier in the day, driving in the pasture on the opposite side of the creek, we had seen a mother goat with two baby kids. Was one of them injured? Had it become separated from its mother? It was time for action. We took a canoe across the creek and I clambered out onto the slippery bank. Climbing up in the darkness toward the faint cry, I found the baby goat, which had lost its footing and fallen from the heights above. As I cradled it in my arms, I could feel its still-wet umbilical cord. Unless reunited with its mother, this frightened animal would die. When I reached the top, I didn't see the mother goat but assumed she was watching from a safe distance. With a silent prayer, I released the baby before climbing down and paddling back across the creek. The following morning we saw the baby goat with its mother. The exhilaration I felt after this rescue mission helped me to understand the shepherd's joy. I had found a lost one! I had saved a life! I was eager to rejoice with friends and neighbors, like the shepherd in the parable. Unfortunately, my "friends and neighbors" consisted of a houseful of teenagers who looked at me warily.

This episode gave me a glimpse into the heart and character of our rescuing God. Devoted, watchful, passionate about "his own." His deliverance is based on grace and unconditional love and not on the worthiness of the lost. He doesn't chide, rebuke, or hate the lost one. He pursues with haste and persistence. He doesn't analyze the reasons the person became lost, because his nature is simply to save and deliver. And he carries us safely home when our strength is spent.

As rescuer of our souls, God is our hero. Can we know him? Is he personal? Bette Midler's lyrics come to mind: "A beautiful face without a name. Did you ever know that you're my hero?" A story about a young Marine in World War II will shed some light on this. Wounded in the battle of Guadalcanal by Japanese machine gun fire, my father-in-law, Baine Kerr, was carried out of the jungle by four men. An iconic photograph shows Baine, his face visible as his head is propped up on his helmet, being carried out of the jungle by these four grizzled Marine stretcher-bearers. These men were rescuers; they were heroes. They carried this wounded Marine away from danger to a place of safety, where he could get medical treatment, be healed, and live. Baine had deep gratitude for these men. But who were they? Sixty years after the war he couldn't recall their names nor did he know if they'd survived the war, which lasted another two and a half years after Guadalcanal. Baine's memoir of his wartime experiences, co-written with John, was published just a year before his death. On the jacket of the book, titled *Only a Khaki Shirt*, is the photograph of the four Marines carrying Baine from the jungle after he'd been shot. Not long after Baine's death in 2008, a young man in Missouri who had come across a copy of the memoir tracked down John. "My grandfather," the young man explained, "was one of the Marines carrying your father in the photograph on the cover of your book." Finally, one of the rescuers had a name.

Our rescuer has a name: Jesus Christ. He is the seeking shepherd who lifts us up when we are wounded and carries us away from danger to safety, so we can be healed, so we can live.

> From shifting sands He lifted me
> With his own hands, He lifted me
> From shades of night to realms of light.[38]

A lamb who has strayed, a baby goat who has fallen, a soldier who has been wounded. What do these stories tell us about the reasons we become lost and in need of God's deliverance and rescue? I see the lamb in Jesus' parable as a more intentional departure from the provision and protection of the shepherd, a form of rejecting God. Enticed by greener pastures, it wanders away in an attitude of independence. Having "tasted the goodness of the word of God," it has fallen away (Heb. 6:5–6). The baby goat represents those who have become lost in a more unintentional, innocent way. Out of careless neglect, he has drifted. In following, he has not followed closely enough. Because he has not realized how dangerously close he has come to the precipice, he loses his footing and falls. And, the young Marine is wounded while simply doing his duty, in combat with the enemy. When we are "wounded in action," simply in the course of our lives, we must cry out for deliverance as David does in the Psalms. The enemy appears in many forms—abuse, addiction, depression, mental or physical illness, or poverty. And we are left feeling powerless to save ourselves.

We cry out for rescue, deliverance, and salvation. We know theologically Christ has accomplished these in his death on the cross. And we are grateful and overwhelmed by God's rescue mission. But what does it look like now in the midst of pain and suffering from which we desire to be delivered? An immature faith believes God to be a genie in a bottle. With enough prayer and petition, God is bound to intervene. If the answer does not come as we have prayed, we doubt and despair and question our faith. God's nature is always to deliver and save, but we must be open to see it in different ways. His miracle of rescue may simply derive from recognizing his presence, from which flows a feeling of peace, patience, and acceptance. We will realize that in the midst of fear, confusion, or peril, his strength is present in our weakness. In our role as the ambassadors of Christ, we must be available to be the hands and feet of God's rescue mission, partnering with him to seek the lost, to encourage the fallen and carry the wounded.

Our fall from God can be willful and intentional or it can be innocent and careless. When we do wander and our foot slips, when we fall from the heights, what does God do?

- When we fall, he comes running.
- When we fall from grace into self-effort, he runs to rescue us.
- When we fall from success to failure, he runs to rescue us.
- When we fall from happiness to depression, he runs to rescue us.
- When we fall from calm to chaos, he runs to rescue us.
- When we fall from contentment to anxiety, he runs to rescue us.

He hears our cry. He does not count the cost. He just runs and lifts us and carries us until we are strong enough to stand again. He reaches down from on high and draws us out of mighty waters (Ps. 18:16). He brings us into a broad place and sets us secure on the heights.

PRAYER

Father, because you loved the world, you sent Jesus on a rescue mission. To hear our cries of distress when we are wounded. To be our stretcher bearer. To lift us into your arms and carry us away from danger. To carry us home. So we can be healed. And live. Did you ever know that you're my hero?

WHERE IS WALDO?

'You will seek me and find me when you seek me with all your heart. I will be found by you,' declares the Lord.

—Jeremiah 29:13–14

My children loved the *Where Is Waldo?* books when they were young. It was a challenge for them to see Waldo on every page as he was cleverly hidden among hundreds of colorful characters and objects. Locating Waldo amid this visual chaos required perseverance, focus, tenacity, and skills of observation. An impatient child would turn the pages too quickly and never find Waldo, often becoming weary, discouraged, or bored. He might have heard the voice of a skeptical sibling (probably the same one who had informed him that there was no Santa Claus!). Haven't you found Waldo yet? Where is Waldo now? You have been tricked! Waldo is not on every page!

Do you remember the excitement when the child's effort was rewarded and he had located Waldo? I see him! There he is! At the completion of the book—with the advantage of experience, practice, and hindsight—the child could go back to the beginning and quickly find Waldo. He remembered what he had seen before. In words sung by Taylor

Swift, "What you been lookin' for was there all along." Beginning a new book in the series, the child was confident that he would find Waldo on every page. The skeptics and naysayers had been wrong.

As we look for God on the pages of our life story, are we like the child searching for Waldo? Is God's presence obvious or obscure amid the chaos, clutter, and myriad distractions? Do we become discouraged when we don't clearly see God's hand in our circumstances? As we turn the pages, is it easier to see God on days of celebration, joy, peace, contentment, and happiness? Does it seem that God was hiding on the pages of tragedy, death, suffering, and pain? The voice of the skeptic taunts us: "Where is your God? Where is he now? Why hasn't he answered your prayer?" Perhaps, if we look more closely on those pages, we will recognize his face in the kindness of friends, the hope of his Word, the comfort and strength of his indwelling Spirit. As I come to the pages of my indifference, the pages of my sin, the pages of my selfishness and anger, I almost hope he was not present at those times.

To see God, perhaps it is not enough to have the qualities of the child who succeeded in seeing Waldo—focus, tenacity, perseverance, and expectation. John the Baptist reveals another characteristic that might help us to see God—the quality of humility.

John saw Jesus coming toward him, passing by, standing and dwelling among men. John was the first to recognize Jesus as the "Lamb of God, who takes away the sin of the world" (Jn. 1:29). Because of John's humility, he clearly understood his role—to be a witness to the Light, to be the voice calling to make a straight way for the Lord, to reveal Jesus to Israel. John always pointed to Jesus so others could follow him. He had no ego or personal agenda for fame that would have prevented his seeing. He knew he was NOT the Christ, or Elijah, or the Prophet. He was aware of his unworthiness even to untie the thong of Jesus' sandal, and supremely aware of the worthiness of the one to whom he points, the one who "has surpassed me because he was before me" (Jn. 1:30).

Can an attitude of humility help us see Jesus on the pages of our life story? Conversely, is pride a barrier that prevents us from seeing intersections of grace and "trees full of angels"?[39] Does pride prevent us from recognizing when we stand on holy ground because "the arrogant cannot stand in your presence"? (Ps. 5:5).

A. W. Tozer writes of the need for humility and the danger of pride. He reasons that although the veil that separated us from God has been removed and the door opened so we have direct access to a Holy God, a veil remains that hides the face of God from us. "We have but to look into our own hearts and we shall see it there, sewn and patched and repaired it may be . . . woven of the fine threads of the self-life, the hyphenated sins of the human spirit."[40] The veil is created by a prideful attitude that we recognize in familiar terms beginning with the word *self*: self-righteousness, self-absorbtion, and self-sufficiency.

Pride did not stand in the way of John the Baptist's ability to see Jesus. Does it affect our ability to see Jesus on the pages of our story? Where is Jesus?

- ☀ Pride looks at a page and says, *I was strong.* Humility points to Jesus who transformed my weakness.
- ☀ Pride looks at a page and says, *I was brave.* Humility points to Jesus who transformed my fear.
- ☀ Pride looks at a page and says, *I was kind.* Humility points to Jesus who transformed my selfishness.
- ☀ Pride looks at a page and says, *I was peaceful.* Humility points to Jesus who transformed my anxiety.
- ☀ Pride looks at a page and says, *I was wise.* Humility points to Jesus who transformed my foolishness.

At the church I attend in San Antonio there is a narrow hallway, called Preacher's Alley, through which the pastor walks to enter the sanctuary to reach the pulpit.

On a beam above the door are the words, "Sir, we would like to see Jesus" (Jn. 12:21). The beam is so low that a preacher must bow his head before entering the sanctuary to preach God's Word. What a beautiful picture. With heads bowed in humility, we will see Jesus and be able to point him out to others.

PRAYER

Father, give us an attitude of humility so we can find you on the pages of our life story. Many people are in a chapter of their life they would like to skim or speed read. They would like to turn the pages quickly in hopes of finding a happy ending, a light at the end of a tunnel of grief, suffering, anxiety, or loneliness. And for those who can't discern your involvement in their present circumstance, I pray for someone to come along and point to you passing by, coming toward them, or standing nearby, and proclaim: "Look, there he is!"

EIGHTEEN

A REMODELING JOB

For we are . . . God's building.

—1 Corinthians 3:9

And we are [God's] house.

—Hebrews 3:4

God is the builder of everything.

—Hebrews 3:4

We live in an old house, built in 1924. Although the foundation remains strong and solid, the house has needed repairs and refurbishing over the years. Our most challenging and frustrating project was the remodeling of our kitchen, something fresh and new created within an existing structure. The idea for this remodeling project originated with the contractor who has helped us for the past twenty years. He said that an updated kitchen would increase the value of our house. We reacted to the idea of transformation with resistance and reluctance. Too much time, too much money, too much trouble.

We were somewhat surprised by his suggestion because we didn't think our kitchen was really *that* bad. We had obviously become accustomed to its quirks, flaws, shortcomings, and imperfections: the missing knobs, the crooked cabinets, and the slanted floor. We were obviously complacent, content, and comfortable with mediocrity.

However, we finally recognized the need for change. We decided to trust the skill of the builder to bring the project to completion and to trust the vision of the architect. This was "a time to tear down and a time to build . . . a time to keep and a time to throw away" (Eccles. 3:3–6). As you might imagine, it did take more time and cost more money than we had anticipated. Our relationship with the contractor was strained. If you had read a newspaper headline, "Irate housewife murders contractor," it would have been me. And instead of Bible study, you might have done prison ministry, bringing cookies for me and my fellow inmates.

As I embarked on the preparatory work of emptying twenty years of accumulated stuff, I sensed that God had something to teach me through this most un-holy experience. I discovered the category of the "under-used"—things purchased for a special recipe and used only one time—Bovril, anchovy paste, hoisin sauce, saffron threads. Other items were useless because the "best used by" dates were years in the past and had to be thrown out. They represented wasted and missed opportunities. The category of "unrealized-potential" was seen in the freezer-burned hatch chilies and leftover turkey from 2006. What plans I'd had for these things! Southwestern macaroni and cheese, turkey hash served on waffles. Ice crystals had formed on my good intentions. And the excess of my pantry made me wonder if I were a secret hoarder. Ten kinds of mustard, twelve varieties of pasta and rice, five types of flour, numerous sets of salt and pepper shakers, and countless spices and seasonings. And from the dark recess of the corner cabinet emerged the forgotten, the neglected. As I brought these items into the light of day, I could evaluate their usefulness. Would they be a component of the new kitchen?

I began to hear "voices in the clutter."[41] Or perhaps I was hearing one voice in this time of deciding what to keep and what to throw away. Might the remodeling of a kitchen parallel God's work of renovating the human heart? Does he encounter the obstacle of our resistance and reluctance to his desire for transformation? Will we embrace the idea of

"Sweet Holy change?"[42] What warnings and challenges had I learned from emptying my kitchen?

Like the once-used saffron threads, we can underutilize God's Word by incorporating it into our lives only at times of crisis or emergency but ignore it when life settles down to normal. We use the Scripture for Bible study; we hear it preached on Sunday but might neglect it on other days. We may reserve God for a certain time of day but be dull to his presence in the remaining hours. To add freshness and quality to our lives, we must take his Word off the pantry shelf and allow it to enhance the flavor of each day by frequent use.

Some opportunities may have a best-used-by date on them. A time to encourage, to speak of our faith, or to invite someone to church or Bible study. These particular moments may not have a long shelf life. There may be an expiration date. The moment passes. It may have been our only chance. Take advantage of those moments when they come your way.

God knows the plans he has for us (Jer. 29:11), just as I had plans for the hatch chilies and leftover turkey. He sees the potential within each of us and he intends to bring it to fruition. Part of his plan is to bless us so we can be a blessing to others. If ice crystals form on our good intentions, none of his people will reach their potential.

The excess of my pantry inspired a desire for simplicity in the new kitchen. With too many choices and too many distractions, we lose focus in our spiritual life. Our numerous Bibles and shelves full of Christian books can be overwhelming. Notice that the primary message of the Scripture often comes in simple form: Christ was dead; Christ is alive. Repent, be baptized, and receive the Holy Spirit. Notice the simplicity of the invitation: Come and see. And the simplicity of witness: I was blind but now I see.

And what is hidden in the corner cabinet of our lives, in the place where things can't be seen? It might be sin. It might be a gift or talent we are reluctant to use. We must bring the forgotten and the neglected into the light of Christ to be evaluated. This is a time to bring our forgotten or hidden sins, our neglected kindnesses into the light of his mercy and forgiveness. What to keep? What to throw away?

Finally, the remodeling of the kitchen was complete (contractor still alive). We admired the new creation. We are called new creations in Christ. Our kitchen is not perfect, and neither are we. Something will break and need repairs. Is there a way to protect and nurture this newness so that the vision of the Architect and the work of the Builder will not have been in vain? The answers to these questions became evident when we moved back into the kitchen, a time to unpack, a time to put away.

Our new high-tech kitchen has many conveniences for efficiency. But I will probably never learn to use many of these things, thus not availing myself of the benefits they offer. The owner's manuals, stacked neatly in a cabinet, will never be read. In Christ we are blessed with every spiritual blessing in the heavenly places (Eph. 1:3), all the "bells and whistles" the Builder could provide for his house. We do not grasp the magnitude, nor do we avail ourselves of the benefit and power that are offered in these many blessings. If I will take the Owner's Manual off the shelf and read its instructions daily, I will begin to live in the newness that is possible in Christ.

This new creation is possible because "the old has gone"(2 Cor. 5:17). But old habits die slowly. We used to keep the trash can in the pantry, but its new location is in an easy-glide pullout cabinet on the other side of the kitchen. Several times a day, I turn to the pantry to throw away a piece of trash. Why do we repeatedly turn to old places of trash and garbage? We remain old houses by clinging to familiar habits and patterns of behavior, refusing to throw out cherished sins.

When I had unpacked and put away everything in the new kitchen, some drawers and cabinets were empty, because we had eliminated the excess. I wanted to protect those empty places, resisting my tendency to quickly fill them again with clutter. To be Christ's new house, I must do the same—nurture and protect the empty spaces for prayer and worship, meditation, and fellowship with God.

God is in the remodeling business, creating something new and fresh within existing structures—individuals and churches. What is our reaction to God's idea of transforming us? Are we resistant and reluctant as John and I were to the idea of remodeling our kitchen? Too much time, too much trouble, too costly. We may not see ourselves as "old houses," broken and in need of repair. We have rationalized that we are not *that* bad, having become comfortable and accommodated to our own quirks, flaws, and shortcomings. Complacent, and content with mediocrity. Unless we trust the design of the Architect and have confidence that the Builder will complete his project, we will remain "ever less than [his] design of [us]."[43]

In this process of transformation, be aware that God transforms from the inside out. He is not a decorator who applies a surface coat of pretty paint—the paint of good deeds or nice behavior. No, God's remodeling is like a stain or a dye that penetrates and permeates, a change that is permanent and visible.[44]

Whether the remodeling is of a kitchen or a human heart, becoming new is a process. The branch needs continual pruning, the field must be ploughed up and replanted, and God's building will need repeated transformation. Paul's admonition to "be transformed by the renewing of your mind" (Rom. 12:2) implies a continuing process. Let God do some internal "renovation of the heart," some remodeling of attitudes, thoughts, habits, and behavior.[45] Perhaps it is time to think about transformation, a "time to tear down and a time to build . . . a time to keep and a time to throw away" (Eccles. 3:3–6).

PRAYER

Father, you see us as new creations, but we hinder this reality. We often do feel like old houses, broken and in need of repair. Help us to trust your design, have faith in your blueprint, and allow the Builder to restore and renew. We want to embrace the newness in the fullness it offers by keeping empty spaces for worship, prayer, and study. We will read the Owner's Manual daily. We will turn away from old places of trash and we will bring our hidden faults and our wasted talents into your light. Help us to answer your call to be learners with our hearts open to change and enlightenment. We are ready for "home improvement" and a "joint, lifelong venture" with you.[46]

NINETEEN

FAILED DOG

My deepest awareness of myself is that I am deeply loved by Jesus Christ and I have done nothing to earn it or deserve it.
—Brennan Manning[47]

You do not stay angry forever but delight to show mercy. You will again have compassion on us.
—Micah 7:18–19

Billy Sunday, an American evangelist, proposed a formula for the ideal Christian life: "Hit the sawdust trail, fall on your knees, and receive Christ as your Savior. Then walk out of this tent into the street, get run over by a Mack truck, and go straight to heaven." Eugene H. Peterson further elaborates: "There is no time to backslide, no temptations to bother with, no doubts to wrestle with . . . no enemies to love, no more sorrow, no more tears. Instant eternity."[48]

All of us have followed part of Billy Sunday's formula—we have fallen on our knees and received Christ as our Savior. But because we have not been hit by the Mack truck, and have not yet gone to heaven, we backslide, we are tempted, and we have doubts and feel sorrow. We struggle in this journey of loving, trusting, following, serving, and obeying God. Sometimes we do okay. Sometimes we fail—missing the mark, falling short.

We remember playing "Mother, may I?" when we were little children on the playground. One step forward, two steps back. Never making any discernable progress.

How grateful we are that Scripture shows us the mistakes, failures, confusion, fear, selfishness, even stupidity of the spiritual giants of the Bible. In the Gospels we learn that Peter shared our struggles. God's "strategy [is] to demonstrate that the great, significant figures in the life of faith were fashioned from the same clay as the rest of us."[49] Using "such poor material would redound to God's greater glory."[50]

You must be wondering why the title of this chapter is "Failed Dog." Let me introduce you to Bridget, a Schnauzer who joined our family three summers ago. We picked her up from a breeder outside Atlanta on our way to our summer home in North Carolina. Thus began our adjustment period. The fenced yard has kept our other dogs safely within its confines—until Bridget. The first week, she paced the boundary of the fence. By the second week, she had found a way of escape. We noticed her sitting outside the fence, looking in. Her expression seemed to convey, "I think I know how I got out, but I sure don't know how to get back. Help me. Bring me home."

After Bridget's third Houdini escape, my husband expressed his frustration. "This isn't going to work. She'll ruin our vacation. She will run away, we will always be worried and always looking for her. We will just have to take her back to the breeder." Under his breath, he muttered the words, "Failed dog."

Aren't we grateful that God does not have the same attitude with us? God shaking his head, saying, "Tsk, tsk, tsk, this is not going to work out. I give up. She is not a keeper." And muttering under his breath, "Failed human."

Peter failed. Nonetheless, God would still use Peter for his glory. To appreciate how God uses flawed and failed humans (and dogs), we need to know Peter's story from the Gospel accounts, Acts of the Apostles and 1 and 2 Peter.

"The *now* is only a thin slice of who we are . . . the before is the root system of the visible now. Our lives cannot be read as newspaper reports on current events. They are unabridged novels with character and plot development, each paragraph essential for mature appreciation."[51]

The "now" Peter, who had been transformed at Pentecost when he received the Holy Spirit, stands up as a leader who speaks boldly, a man who is steadfast and strong. In John's Gospel, we see a different Peter. After Jesus' arrest in the Garden of Gethsemane, Peter is hiding in the shadows, shaking in his sandals, and denying his relationship with Jesus. In his epistle, Peter uses the phrase "mists driven by a storm" (2 Pet. 2:17), a visual picture of weakness as the terrifying circumstances swirled around him.

Peter's story is also our story. Let's join him as he warms himself by the fire in the courtyard of the high priest. Peter is about to utter words he will regret for the rest of his life. "I am not one of them . . . I was not in the Garden with him . . . I don't know him." Surely each of us remembers and regrets a careless or hurtful word that disappointed a friend when he or she needed our support and encouragement.

Failed dog. Failed human. Words of condemnation and judgment. At times it is the voice of other people; sometimes the voice is our own. Jesus wants us to move beyond the guilt and remorse we feel after failure. He can still use us for his glory and purpose.

There is more to learn from Bridget's story. Because of the love, determination, and commitment of her masters, Bridget moved beyond being a "F.D." Forgiven, saved, redeemed, and given a second chance. Because of the same qualities in our Master, we can move beyond our failures. We are also forgiven, saved, redeemed, and given a second chance. The Master carries us home, looks at us in love, and comforts us with an outstretched arm. Shall we "put some meat on those bones?" (Pardon the pun!)

The Master Carries Us Home

Bridget must have sensed the implication of being called "F.D." The next morning she showed me her route of escape. Looking over her shoulder to be sure I was watching, she led me to a hole in the fence behind the tool shed and walked out of the yard into the driveway. I picked her up in my arms and brought her back. This process was repeated three times. I think she was saying, "Don't let me go."

Like Bridget's wanderings, leaving God may be easy, but we can't always remember how to get home. Sin creates a fence that separates us from God. But God is the shepherd who seeks the strays and brings them back (Ezek. 34). When we are too weary and weak to find our way, he carries us on eagles' wings and brings us back safely again to his backyard (Exod. 19:4). We barricaded Bridget's escape route so she could no longer get away, determined not to lose her. God assures us that "not one that the Father has given to Jesus will be lost." We are held in his hand. He will not let us run away.

The Master Looks at Us in Love

The night Bridget was condemned as "failed dog," I gave her a look to assure her that I still loved her. We will work this out together to make her a better puppy.

After Peter denied Jesus the third time, the rooster crowed and the Lord turned and looked at him (Lk. 22:61). He looked at Peter in the same way God looks at us when we fail, "as God has looked at His creatures through the aeons: disappointment without end weighed against inexhaustible love."[52]

The Master Comforts Us with Outstretched Arms

Bridget's kennel was by my side of the bed. All night I slept with my arm outstretched over the edge of the bed to give her the assurance that I was nearby and my love for her had not changed, in spite of her failure. (The next morning, my right arm was three inches longer than the left, and I had to have a massage to ease the pain.)

The outstretched arm and mighty hand of God are powerful images in Scripture. God's mighty hand is an expression of his sovereign power and dominion. The outstretched arm represents God's support and strength as he helps his failed children reach their potential. The Hebrew word for *arm* derives from the root word for *seed*, indicating future growth through the gradual process by which God perfects his people.

Bridget failed. Peter failed. We all have failed. Adam and Eve's failure is referred to as the fall of man. We fall from grace, we fall short, and we fall apart. In the book *Half Broke Horses*, a five-year-old child is learning to ride horseback. Her many falls terrified her mother but her father told her, "[The] most important thing in life . . . is learning how to fall."[53] When we fail and feel we have fallen from grace, we need to know that underneath are the everlasting arms, waiting to catch us, pick us up, and set us on our feet again.

We may not live up to Billy Sunday's formula for the ideal Christian life. We will have times when we backslide, we will struggle with temptation, and we will have doubts and sorrow. But because Christ is our Savior, we look forward to eternal life with no more sorrow and no more tears. In heaven, we will not hear the words "failed dog" or "failed human."

PRAYER

Father, we thank you that in our worst failures, your promises remain true, your peace is still offered, and your presence is still assured. You carry us home when we have wandered. You still look at us in love as your treasured possession. Your arm is stretched out to comfort us and give us endurance for the journey. When we fall, we fall into your arms. We can say, like Peter, "In his great mercy he has given us new birth into a living hope" (1 Pet. 1:3). When we have failed, when we have fallen away from your purpose, you are there to save, redeem, and forgive. No longer do we have to think of ourselves as "failed humans."

TWENTY

THE WISE GUYS

Do not forsake wisdom, and she will protect you.
—Proverbs 4:6

If any of you lacks wisdom, you should ask God.
—James 1:5

The Proverbs of King Solomon were written to teach us about "wisdom," a word that appears forty-six times in this book of the Bible. Because wisdom "calls aloud, . . . [to] raise her voice in the public square" (Prov. 1:20), it is considered an attainable goal.

Wisdom is one of God's attributes. Although its fullness is found only in him, Scripture makes it clear that God wants us to be wise also. Let's amend our New Year's resolutions: less sugar, more wisdom. That would be a wise thing!

The *wisemen.* I say the words so fast that I have never paid much attention to the fact that these were wise men, men of wisdom. I greet my neighbor, Mr. Goodman, never thinking that the family name derived from good man. Is he a good man? We live near the University of the Incarnate Word in San Antonio, Texas. I exercise there. I like the Christmas lights at Incarnate Word. Precious words I repeat so frequently they have become commonplace—like saying, "Pass the butter"! To recapture their significant meaning, perhaps we should refer to this university as "the

University of the Word Became Flesh and Dwelt Among Us." And Trinity University, in San Antonio? "God in Three Persons University" might be better.

Back to the wise men. What was it about these "Three Kings of Orient" that made them wise? And what can we learn from them, as we strive to become wise women? The first thing they did was to notice the "star of wonder, star of night, star of royal beauty bright." In fact, they observed his star at its rising. In the early dawn, Venus, the morning star, is still sparkling in the darkness, the brightest object in the sky aside from the moon and the sun. A wise woman, upon her daily rising, will first notice Jesus, the "bright Morning Star" (Rev. 22:16), before she tackles the obligations and responsibilities of her day.

After noticing the star, the three kings were not content just to ponder, discuss, and study the mystery. Staying in the same place was not an option—they had to see firsthand. Wisdom propelled them to ". . . traverse afar. Field and fountain, moor and mountain following yonder star."[54] A wise woman will always be journeying closer to the Christ child, closing any distance that has crept in—understanding that movement toward him is often a movement away from something else.

The wise men asked the right question: "Where is the child?" Ironically, the scribes knew the prophecy of Micah that the ruler of Israel would come from Bethlehem. But the scribes' knowledge did not inspire them to seek the child. The wise woman should also be asking, "Where is the child?" Is he in my heart? Am I nurturing his growth inside me? Do I see him in his Word? Is he evident in my attitudes, actions, thoughts, and speech? Do we look for the child in the people we encounter every day? Our knowledge about the child should always inspire us to seek him.

The wise men understood the identity of the child, "born a King on Bethlehem's plain . . . King forever, ceasing never."[55] We also acknowledge Jesus as King, but act as if there is room on the throne for both of us. The woman of wisdom will pray "thy Kingdom come" with the force of the Spanish translation, *Venga tu reino*—Come, thy

Kingdom! This is a true invitation for Jesus to be Lord of our life.

The woman of wisdom should react as the wise men did when they found the child. Overwhelming joy, "prayer and praising, all men raising, worship him, God on high."[56] And they opened their treasures: "Gold I bring to crown him again." Of course, we need to offer God the treasures of our time, talent, and resources. But we must understand that God considers us to be his "treasured possession." He wants an authentic relationship with those that are open to "divine breathings, divine prompting, divine power."[57] And finally, the wise men "returned to their country by another route" (Mt. 2:12). An encounter with Christ should always lead the wise woman to travel a road of different choices and decisions.

Wisdom is a theme that is continued in the New Testament. Paul prays that God will give the Ephesians "a Spirit of wisdom as they come to know him," and James encourages us that anyone lacking in wisdom should ask God who gives to all generously (Jas. 1:5). We need to pray that God will show us the way to his wisdom. God can speak to us in surprising ways. Had his guidance come in a *Better Homes and Gardens* article titled "Girls of Wisdom"? When women were asked what items they would require if stranded on a desert island, their list of essentials included lip balm, an iPad, a shirt with built-in sunscreen, a yogurt mask, lavender oil, long-lasting mascara, wet wipes, and face cleanser. Certainly, we can aspire to a deeper wisdom than that.

As I continued to think about wisdom, I wondered why we credit an owl with this attribute. In ancient Greece, the owl was associated with Athena, the Greek goddess of wisdom. In modern times, a nursery rhyme helps explain the wisdom of the owl:

> A wise old owl lived in an oak;
> The more he heard, the less he spoke;
> The less he spoke, the more he heard.
> Why can't we be like that wise old bird?[58]

God used a wise old owl to teach me something. Going outside in the early morning, I see the light of Venus is still shining through the winter branches of our leafless pecan tree, "bare ruined choirs, where late the sweet birds sang."[59] I turn my first thoughts to Jesus and begin to pray for people who are suffering grief, illness, disappointment, failure—the list goes on. And I realize that as much as they want to be "guided to thy perfect light," they may not notice anything but the darkness. Green leaves and singing birds seem a distant memory, and they wonder when new life and spring will come. Like the tangle of limbs and twigs of our pecan tree, their lives may seem a confusion of challenges, obstacles, and problems. They may be asking God: *What* is going on? *When* will my situation change? *Why* did this happen to me? *Where* is God? *How* can I handle this?

At that moment, I heard the hoot of the owl that lives in our neighborhood, and the wisdom of the owl became clear. He is always saying, "Who Who." Instead of our Why Why? When When? Where Where? How How?

- ✦ When we ask *why*, our answer should be: look to Jesus *who* was and is and evermore shall be.
- ✦ When we ask *when*, our answer should be, look to Jesus *who* was and is and evermore shall be.
- ✦ When we ask *where* and *how*, our answer should be to look to Jesus, *who* was and is and evermore shall be.

We are on the road to wisdom when we know that our questions will always find their answer in the *Who*, the person of Jesus Christ, our own bright Morning Star, the brightest light in the heaven, brighter than the sun, the moon, and even Venus.

F ather, help us to learn the wisdom of the Magi— to notice you, to follow your light, to seek you diligently even if the journey is long. Help us to ask the right question: "Where is the Child" in my life? We want to live in acknowledgment that you are King. We want to be joyful and worship you, to open the treasure that is our heart. And we want to be willing to travel a different road. As we grow in wisdom we will know that when life is dark, or barren and empty, or just too confusing, your light is always shining. The brightest light in the heaven, "the One from whom all darkness flees."[60]

TWENTY-ONE

GOD'S BIOGRAPHIES

"All the days ordained for me were written in your book
before one of them came to be."
—Psalm 139:16

In Scripture, God is referred to as Author. Jesus is
called the "author of life" (Acts 3:15). God-inspired writers
recorded poetry, history, and compelling narrative. Some
of the biblical accounts make you think God also enjoys
story telling—a talking donkey, Jonah in the whale, a staff
that becomes a snake, the parting of the Red Sea—to name
a few. But his favorite genre is biography, stories that cover every aspect of your life, beginning before you were
born (Ps. 139:16). The world's largest library, the Library of
Congress, has 118 million items and 500 miles of shelf space.
That sounds impressive until you compare it with the
library of heaven, which contains a book for every person
who ever lived. Even the most renowned biographers can't
be compared with the biographer, God.

Because my husband is a writer, I have observed what
is involved in completing a story. When John begins a new
novel, he has already figured out the ending. The task

requires perseverance, hard work, optimism, and love of the process. He has a plan to bring his characters to the completion he has imagined for them. And on the way to that conclusion, the protagonist often experiences a crisis or turning point, followed by transformation, even redemption. John would be disappointed if the reader judged one of his characters before finishing the novel.

Using the metaphor of punctuation, God's biographies contain many chapters and volumes because he includes all the cycles of crisis and turning points that occur in our lives. God's choice of punctuation is significant. He uses lots of commas and semicolons to indicate that the story continues beyond a crisis. He keeps writing the story until his character comes to a point of transformation and redemption.

If Satan were writing our life story, his would be a CliffsNotes or the *Reader's Digest Condensed Books* version. He enjoys punctuating with a period, full stop, at the moment his character experiences a time of crisis, suffering, pain, or tragedy. Period, the end, story is over. There is no hope, no future, and no light at the end of the tunnel. Satan's version of some biblical accounts would look like this:

> Abraham and Sarah were too old to conceive a
>   child. Period! The end!
> God's people were enslaved in Egypt for 400 years.
>   Period! The end!
> Peter denied Jesus for the third time and the
>   rooster crowed. Period! The end!
> Jesus cried from the cross, "It is finished." Period!
>   The end!
> The early church experienced great persecution
>   and all were scattered. Period! The end!

Satan doesn't like to write about second chances that create the opportunity for transformation. He prefers that we read only the first scene or chapter of a book and make a quick judgment. He is delighted when we decide someone is simply a bad read and put the book aside, the person judged, condemned, and then forgotten.

In the first chapter of the book *Olive Kitteridge*, a collection of thirteen related short stories by Elizabeth Strout, I saw Olive as resentful, unkind, selfish, cruel to her husband, and in conflict with her son. I judged the book as a bad read. I wanted nothing more to do with Olive. Even the author admitted to needing a break from her. But even someone like Olive deserves a second chance. Having decided to finish the book, I gained a better understanding of Olive as she interacted with a variety of people and responded to challenging situations. I alternately hated her, pitied her, admired her, and at times identified with her. But she had won my compassion and empathy. *Olive Kitteridge* had been a good read after all.

Unfortunately, we are prone to making quick judgments about people—not just fictional characters like Olive. This tendency to judge someone in the first chapter of our acquaintance was exemplified in a *New York Times* article suggesting that a person's character and personality could be revealed from the kind of sandwich he orders! Is Satan writing for the *New York Times*? The next time I succumbed to the temptation to judge a stranger as a bad read, period, God used an unusual way to remind me to punctuate with a comma. Bad read, comma, try again.

In our Central Market food emporium, I was in a hurry. Like Mario Andretti at the Indianapolis 500, I raced down the aisles causing cans and cereal boxes to fall off the shelves in the wake of my speeding cart. I arrived at the deli counter out of breath. There is a truth you must know: the deli counter is the invention and tool of Satan. Time at the deli counter "tries men's souls."[61] There are no fruits of the Spirit at the deli counter. Love, joy, peace, patience, and self-control have been left behind in the produce section among the kiwis, strawberries, and melons.

This was July fifth. Everything in the deli counter was on sale. A male customer was ordering one slice of everything, from ham to turkey to prosciutto—the list continued. And he was enjoying a leisurely chat with the deli employee! The only Christian behavior I could muster was to walk away. I came back. Nothing had progressed. The slicing and chatting continued. Maybe I needed to return to the produce department and get the fruit of patience.

Miraculously, heaven was unzipped and a sprinkling of grace, like pixie dust, must have descended over this scene. I heard the customer say that he shops and cooks for his elderly parents. That's nice. I looked at him. Kind eyes and a gentle expression. To my surprise, I found myself talking to him about my son's upcoming wedding, surely infuriating another crazed shopper. Then I noticed that his left arm was shriveled at the elbow. Thalidomide baby, I guessed. At that moment, he extended his right arm and handed me a business card for "Piano Man," explaining that he is a pianist and has played at the White House and many other functions. I thanked him and walked off in a daze. A one-armed piano player? How can that be? Impossible! When I swiped my credit card to check out, these words appeared on the screen: "Bad read, try again." I know we can hear God's voice in many ways, but this is the first time he has spoken to me through a credit card machine. But I understood the truth, the warning and the challenge of those words.

It could be our own life that we judge as a bad read. As the Author creates, continues, and completes our life story, we may wish we could see the whole picture of our life, which shows how all the random pieces fit together. Haven't you ever been impatient while reading a novel and taken a quick peek at the last chapter? In the same way we may ask God to show us the end of our days. God, what are you doing with this situation? Will it turn out that all things will work together for good? Will God's plans for my life ever come to fruition? As we live the chapters of our lives, it may simply seem puzzling at times.

Our lives may share something in common with the jigsaw puzzles that were a part of my childhood. My parents had many Par custom wooden puzzles, hand carved by Mr. Ware in Manhattan, who began his one-man puzzle factory during the Depression. Packaged in a plain black box, there was no picture to show you what the completed puzzle would look like. Even the title kept you guessing: "Over the Rail," "Butterfly Kisses," and "Above the Crowd." The mystery about the final picture did not mar our contentment in the hours spent putting the puzzle together piece by piece. Because we had worked many of these puzzles, we trusted that the design would be beautiful, as Mr. Ware had never disappointed us before.

Another element of the Par puzzles was that the shape of the puzzle was not always known. It was usually not a straight-edged rectangle, but might be a circle or an oval or have curved edges. If there were straight lines, they might appear in the interior of the puzzle. Mixed in with the hundreds of ordinary pieces were a handful of Par pieces, exquisitely and delicately shaped—perhaps a unicorn, a ballerina, a sailboat, a butterfly, or a hummingbird. When the last piece was put in place, we admired the finished masterpiece and realized that every piece had contributed to its beauty.

God knows how all the chapters of our life story will finally come together. He knows the picture on the box and wants us to be patient as piece by piece our lives are taking shape and acquiring beauty in the process. Like the Par puzzles, we also have a title: Child of God, Treasured Possession, Chosen, Redeemed, Precious in his sight. Who knows, the completed picture might be a one-armed man playing a piano concert at the White House.

Some chapters of our life may seem unremarkable; a few we would like to edit and rewrite. But just like the delight and surprise we had when we came across a Par piece, some chapters of our life give us a deep happiness and joy as we remember them. Some pieces of our life may be considered "under par." Times of sin, bad choices, failure, grief. We may have wanted to give up on the puzzle, tempted to stop reading the story. At these times, we need to remember God's holy punctuation. Don't put a period too soon. God is creating, continuing, and completing your story. And you can be confident of his commitment to take your story through to transformation and redemption.

- After sin, comma, the story continues.
- After bad choices, comma, the story continues.
- After failure, comma, the story continues.
- After grief, comma, the story continues.
- After death, comma, the story continues.

PRAYER

Lord, when we are called to serve you, we are all "one-armed piano players"—limited, deficient, and handicapped in some way. We are quick to use words like impossible, improbable, and unlikely. We can all look back on our lives and see the times we were tempted to give up, deciding there was no future and no hope. We cannot envision the completed picture you have planned. But we trust that when a time of crisis comes and Satan wants to end our story with a period, you will take the pen out of his hand and put a comma. Try again! Your story continues. The pieces are not all in place.

TWENTY-TWO

HOMESICK

My Father's house has many rooms. . . . I am going there to prepare a place for you . . . I will come back and take you to be with me.

—John 14:2–3

It has been said the only two certainties in life are death and taxes. As certain as they are, we try to evade taxes (not really) and avoid death! Peter and Paul seem to have made friends with death, their ministries characterized by courage and boldness because they had no fear or dread of the inevitability of their deaths. Paul is not trying to escape death (Acts 25:11); in fact, he would prefer to die and be with the Lord. Peter eagerly anticipates his future inheritance and the rich welcome he will receive. As we consider the reality of our mortality and the reality of heaven that awaits, we may wonder if "eternity can be conveyed to finite human minds"?[62]

Heaven. Jesus thought of it as his Father's house and as Paradise. He set his face toward Jerusalem and submitted to the agony of the cross to open the way for us to be there with him.

What do we think about this eternal life that Jesus died to secure for us? We use the word *heaven* so frequently that it may have lost its proper sense of awe. When I eat a green enchilada or a bean cup at a favorite Mexican restaurant, I utter, "Yum, this is heaven." The Hinckley Picnic Boat is advertised as "your dream of heaven." (This is an accurate statement for my husband.) A crisp, clear day in the Blue Ridge Mountain elicits "this place is pure heaven." An unexpected blessing that comes our way is heaven-sent. An incredible experience makes us feel we have "died and gone to heaven."

People have different attitudes about eternity. Huck Finn thought it sounded boring. Ted Kennedy would have disagreed. The eulogy at his funeral service said Ted would be having a busy afterlife. Far from boring! George MacDonald in *Diary of an Old Soul*, written the year after two of his adult children died, thought of heaven as a place where his children would be happy, contented, and even having fun. He wrote: "What if thou make us able to make like thee—To light with moons, to clothe with greenery, To hang gold sunsets o'er a rose and purple sea!"[63]

Do we want to be in heaven? Of course we do! Someday. Not now. Not yet. Because God has planted eternity in human hearts (Eccles. 3:11), we are supposed to feel like visitors here, passing through—on the way to our real home. Nonetheless, most of us are enjoying this earthly life—with its blessings and beauty, its abundance of experiences and relationships. We simply are not ready to move to heaven. Our feelings are a bit similar to my daughter's feelings about moving back to San Antonio. She knows it is a good place to live. She values the comfort, love, friends and family, the culture and ambiance. Someday she will be ready to move home. Not now. Not yet.

Some people are ready and eager for heaven, the sooner the better. The oppressed, the persecuted, the enslaved, those exhausted from fighting a long illness, and the elderly who have outlived health are ready to cross the Jordan, looking for those chariots a'comin'. They have the same longing expressed by the writer of Psalm 84: "How lovely is your dwelling place, Lord Almighty! My soul yearns, even faints for the courts of the Lord" (Ps. 84:1–2). Phrases like "dwelling place," "the sparrow finds a home," and "happy are those who live in your house" show that the psalmist thinks of heaven as home and death as a homecoming. This attitude may diminish the sting—the fear and dread most of us have about death.

God must want his children to be a little homesick for their eternal home. The way we felt our first year at summer camp or our freshman year of college. Like E.T., the extraterrestrial creature who pointed his glowing finger toward the sky and wistfully said "Home." Like Dorothy in *The Wizard of Oz,* following the yellow brick road on her determined quest to find her way back to Kansas—home.

Our daughter has not lived in San Antonio since she left for college. Every time she comes for a visit, I spend time preparing her room. At the end of her journey I want it to be a haven of rest and comfort. Continuing a years-long tradition, I place a vase of yellow roses in her room. Because of the song "The Yellow Rose of Texas," we both understand the significance of this gesture. The roses are like Dorothy's yellow brick road intended to foster her longing for home. To entice her, to remind her. London and New York are temporary residences—Texas is your real home. This is who you are, this is where you are from, this is where you belong, this is where you are loved and cherished. Come home.

We understand the homesickness of E.T. and Dorothy. How might we foster a feeling of homesickness for the unknown, invisible reality of heaven? "Immortal, invisible, in light inaccessible, hid from our eyes."[64] "No eye has seen . . . no ear has heard what God has prepared for us" (1 Cor. 2:9). Is it important that we become more heaven-minded while still immersed in the responsibilities, activities, challenges, and pleasures of this life? C. S. Lewis believed that the most effective Christians in this earthly life are those who think the most about heaven and eternity. Perhaps we need to do some pondering of Paradise.

Many mornings, I start my day sitting on an upstairs balcony from which I see my neighbor's stucco wall through the branches of our red oak. Their interior garden on the other side of the wall seemed symbolic of heaven—a safe and protected haven, real but hidden from my eyes. The scent of mountain laurel drifts over their wall. I hear voices, laughter, and sometimes classical music from the other side. Birds fly from my neighbor's garden and perch in my red oak. Squirrels leap easily between the trees in both yards. At night, a soft light illuminates the trees. I was curious to know what lies beyond the wall.

One day the yardman left the wooden gate slightly ajar, affording me a glimpse into this hidden world. In the same way, God prepares us by opening heaven (Mt. 3:16) to give us peeks into paradise, graciously "pulling the veil aside to give us glimpses of the glories to come—a future beyond our wildest dreams, a Story beyond all telling."[65] These tastes of heaven stimulate our longing for our eternal home, for what awaits us on the other side of this earthly life.

One day my neighbor might extend an invitation to come to her home. Taking me by the hand, she will lead me through the gate into her beautiful dwelling. And one day God will take us by the hand so we can be with him where he is. When he leads us through the open gate, I think we will be surprised at how familiar it seems, almost déjà vu, as if we have been there before. An experience I had when we visited our best friends in Vancouver illustrates this. When they lived in San Antonio, we spent many evenings in their home, having dinner, talking, and playing cards. I expected their urban condominium to be very unfamiliar, very different. But when the door opened—there it all was—the same. The pink-and-white striped chintz couch, the large abstract painting of pastel colors. We ate at the same dining table, talked for hours, played cards. And I thought—this is just the way it will be when we get to heaven. Familiar.

I often listen to music on my iPod during my morning quiet time on the upstairs balcony. Following "Fifty Greatest Hymns" is Lee Ann Rimes singing "How Do I Live." Her voice conveys her devotion to the man that she loves, as she contemplates a life without him. The lyrics could be my song to God, "How do I get through one night without you, if I had to live without you, what kind of life would that be . . ."[66] The sentiment of the song continues in the same vein. Her man is the center of her world; without him, there would be nothing good in her life and the sun would no longer shine.

One morning a heaven-sent insight struck me. These are the words God is singing to us, his children. He doesn't want to live without us! We are the "world . . . heart . . . soul"[67] of our *Abba*-Father. He is longing for us to be home with him. He is waiting for the day when Jesus' prayer in John 17:21 is answered: ". . . As you [Father], are in me and I am in you. May they also be in us." This prayer for us to be united eternally with the Father and Son is answered when we die. Death is not the end of our life story. The end of our earthly life is not punctuated with a period, but by a comma, to show that our life continues. The comma is the shape of a cupped hand—God's hand that has held our life from before our birth and will hold us when we die; the hand that will lead us to our new home.

God is homesick for us! He is preparing our room, a haven of comfort and rest. A vase of yellow roses will be there. And we both will understand the significance of that gesture. You have come home. This is where you are loved. This is where you belong—near the heart of the Father.

PRAYER

Father, we cling to the promise of eternal life and the assurance that we will spend eternity looking into your face and reunited with our loved ones. Help us to be more heaven-minded, a little homesick for our eternal home. The door to eternity is the perfect width for two people to walk through together. We will not make that journey alone, but holding the hand of Jesus. The only regret we will have in heaven is that in this life we worried so much and trusted so little. But finally, we will understand the love of God for his children.

TWENTY-THREE

COFFEE WITH THE NATIVITY

Fragile finger sent to heal us,
Tender brow prepared for thorn,
Tiny heart whose blood will save us,
Unto us is born.

—Michael W. Smith

In my early twenties I went on a tour with several other girls to the South Pacific. Down Under, in Australia, the seasons are reversed so that July is winter. We felt that a Christmas celebration was in order so we decorated a small Norfolk pine tree for our hotel room and exchanged gifts. Christmas in July?

Why should the spirit of Christmas be bound to a date on the calendar? One year I celebrated it on December 25 and again in mid-January. Sitting by the fire every morning, I listened to Christmas carols and recaptured the spirit, even with all the Christmas decorations put away, except one.

The Nativity set was still on the refectory table in the front hall. Thinking I might leave it out indefinitely, I replaced the holly and poinsettias with springtime flowers. With "Hark the Herald Angels" playing in the background and the Nativity surrounded by lilacs and lilies, roses and daffodils, I knew that the timeless spirit of Christmas could be celebrated in December, January, April, or July.

I sensed that God was inviting me into the Christmas story in a deeper way than ever before. Over the course of a week in January, I decided to celebrate Christmas a second time. Every morning sitting by the fireplace, I enjoyed a coffee break with each participant in God's divine drama. One by one, I brought the figures from the front hall and placed them on the table by the couch, so I could hear them tell their story.

Monday, Coffee with Mary

Mary told me that when she became betrothed to Joseph, she had begun planning for their future together, the life she had dreamed of—simple, peaceful, predictable, and uncomplicated. But God had a different plan, one for which she had been chosen, one that he wanted to accomplish through her. Mary was troubled and perplexed when the angel Gabriel told her she was to bear a son. This was impossible. She was a virgin. How could she be the one God had chosen to bear the long-awaited great one, the Son of the Most High? Gabriel assured her that God favored her and that he was with her. When the Most High overshadowed her, she learned that nothing is impossible with God. As she submitted to his will, she was able to say, "I am the Lord's servant . . . may your word to me be fulfilled" (Lk. 1:38). She understood, finally, that the Mighty One would do great things for her and she acknowledged his holiness, his mercy, and his strength. And the great miracle would come in a small bundle.

Tuesday, Coffee with Joseph

Joseph requested that instead of Christmas carols he would like to hear a good rendition of "The Impossible Dream." His dreams were shattered when he learned of Mary's pregnancy, knowing he was not the father. After his dreams were shattered, Joseph was comforted by the encouraging words of the angel of the Lord who told him not to be afraid to take Mary as his wife. Joseph chose to obey God and swallow his pride, denying his desire to dismiss her quietly. Conquering his fear, Joseph submitted to God's greater purpose, understanding that his role was to protect the mother and child. God was always waking him, saying, "Get up and take the child." And he did, fleeing to Egypt, returning years later to Judea, and then moving to Galilee where it was safer. Always taking the child as he moved.

Wednesday, Coffee with the Shepherds

They encouraged me to be alert to extraordinary things appearing in the midst of the ordinary. God's glory can appear in the midst of your daily responsibilities, keeping watch over your flocks at night. Don't ignore the interruption. Seeking him now is always more important than tending your sheep. Although a great company of the Heavenly Host announced the Good News convincingly, the shepherds did not want a second-hand faith. They themselves had to see this miracle in order to encounter the Savior personally. Waste no time, make haste to find him! They told me not to be afraid to spread the Word. Our witness is the same as theirs—to praise God and tell people what you have seen and heard.

Thursday, Coffee with the Wise Men

The wise men, with their camels, occupied a lot of space on the coffee table as we shared our coffee break. Travel-weary from their journey from the East, they suggested music by The Seekers to restore their energy. And then, they imparted their wise advice to me. If you have to travel a long distance to find him, seek him still. Though the journey is arduous, seek him still. Seek with diligence, search for him carefully. And when you have found him, get on your knees, worship him, and let joy overwhelm you. Open your treasures and present your gifts before him.

Because there are dangerous forces like Herod in your midst, you may be required to travel "by another road" to protect his precious life.

Friday, Coffee with the Infant God

"The floodgates of heaven have been opened and so much blessing poured out that we don't have room enough for it." These verses from Malachi cause me to marvel that the blessing came as it did. The Infinite came as an infant, the King came as a child, the Warrior was weak, the Deliverer was defenseless, the Creator was crying. This divine baby was vulnerable and helpless, born in humble circumstances, in need of nurture, protection, and love. In his humanity, he is like all babies: difficult to resist and impossible to ignore. Babies occupy your thoughts and energy as they rearrange your life, your schedule, and your priorities. Babies rouse parents from sleep. Is the Christ Child trying to awaken us from a lazy, sleepy discipleship?

Other Voices of the Nativity

Other voices spoke to me that mid-January Christmas. The Star asked if my light shines brightly enough to show someone the way to the Christ Child. The angels asked if I am giving glory to God in the highest, spreading the Good News, reminding people that God's favor rests on them and that he brings peace.

Unexpectedly, I heard a message from two characters never portrayed in a Nativity scene. The innkeeper warns me that daily duties and responsibilities can occupy the room that should be reserved for the Christ Child. The blessing passes by unnoticed if we are too busy. And Simeon inspires me most of all. As he takes the baby Jesus in his arms he praises God, "For my eyes have seen your salvation" (Lk. 2:30). In fact, Simeon feels he could now die in peace because he has seen the light of God's glory. The words of Bach's cantata *Ich habe genug*, first performed in 1727, should touch our hearts deeply. It is translated "I have enough" or "I am content." It begins, "It is enough to have held the Savior, the hope of all peoples in the warm embrace of my arms." Oh, that we could ever find our true contentment, our "enough" in him.

At the end of my week of coffee breaks, each person was placed back on the refectory table. This fellowship that is gathered around the Christ Child stands on holy ground. And they stand on common ground, with each other and with us. Although God called Mary, Joseph, the wise men, and shepherds to this place, they each had a choice to make that would determine if they would play a role in God's plan. They chose to love, serve, obey, trust, protect, proclaim, worship, and listen even when they didn't fully understand the mystery, when they didn't have all the answers. They chose to step away from the familiar, comfortable, explicable, safe, and predictable. They chose to be obedient to God's purpose even though it was not their plan or maybe even their preference. They learned to accept God's will rather than to change it. And they would discover that being in God's perfect will is not a guarantee that the road will be easy. If we will make similar choices, we will find him at the center of our lives. If we don't make these choices, there is a danger that the story of our life will be set to the music of the Drifters.

Like Mary, I choose to let him grow in me, changing the shape of my life. I will treasure and ponder the mystery of her son. Like Mary, we must also carry this baby to full term, but our gestation is not nine months but a lifetime. Love him, and hold him close. Like Joseph, I choose to take the baby with me, protecting his life. Like the wise men, I choose to seek him and lay my gifts before him, finding joy in his presence. Like the shepherds, I choose to rejoice and spread the Good News.

Every day, the promise of Malachi is being fulfilled, the floodgates of heaven are pouring out more blessing than we have room for, because of God's choice to make his dwelling among us. Emmanuel, we praise and worship you.

> What can I give Him, poor as I am?
> If I were a shepherd, I would bring a lamb;
> If I were a Wise Man, I would do my part;
> Yet what can I give Him: give Him my heart.[68]

Emmanuel, God with us, we do give you our hearts. We will keep the spirit of Christmas in December, April, and July, praising you all seasons of the year.

TWENTY-FOUR

MY PEACE I GIVE YOU

The Lord blesses his people with peace.

—Psalm 29:11

*And the peace of God, which transcends all understanding,
will guard your hearts and your minds.*

—Philippians 4:7

Shalom, the Hebrew word for peace, appears more than 230 times in the Old Testament. It signifies completeness, welfare, health, and protection. In the New Testament, it means rest, contentment, and quietness, peace between nations, and a harmonized relationship between God and man, through the shed blood of Jesus.

The Merriam-Webster Dictionary defines *peace* as a "state of tranquility or quiet, freedom from disquieting or oppressive thoughts." But who needs a dictionary? It doesn't really matter if we can define it. We all know when we are at peace or feeling peaceful. Rest in peace! Do we have to wait until we enter the pearly gates, or is it something we can have now?

In Chapter 14 of John's Gospel, Jesus makes several promises, each one a profound gift: the promise of eternal life, the promise of the Holy Spirit, the promise that he will come and make his home with us. And the promise of his peace. Many people have told me that the promise of peace is the one that means the most to them.

Peace. A promise of Jesus and something we desire. A gift he offers us: "Peace I leave with you; my peace I give you" (Jn. 14:27). "Peace" was a parenthesis around Jesus' life, forming bookends from his birth to his death and resurrection. Isaiah prophesied he would be the Prince of Peace, and the angels announced "Peace on Earth" at his birth. Before his death, he promised peace to the disciples, and after the resurrection he greeted them with "Peace be with you."

How does it affect Jesus when we don't accept the gift of his peace?

Twice in the Gospels we see Jesus weep: once at the tomb of Lazarus and the other time when he entered Jerusalem and lamented, "If you, even you, had only known on this day what would bring you peace" (Lk.19:42). As Jesus wept for lack of peace two thousand years ago, so he must grieve today when we are fearful, anxious, or worried because each of these robs us of peace.

Our lack of peacefulness may be due to a misunderstanding of Jesus' kind of peace. Perhaps we need to pay attention to the context in which he offers this gift. Jesus tells his disciples that he gives them a peace that is different from what the world gives. Then he tells them "You will weep and mourn. . . . You will grieve" (Jn. 16:20) because of what they will receive from the world—hatred, persecution, and expulsion from the synagogue. It may surprise us that following this dire forecast Jesus again mentions his peace.

What kind of peace is this? It must be the "peace . . . which transcends all understanding" (Phil. 4:7) that is unrelated to circumstances, a kind of peace that almost does not make sense. This is peace "in the midst of" and "in spite of" your circumstances. It reminds me of the story of the World War I Christmas Eve truce. After months of fighting from their trenches, the soldiers found that the spirit of Christmas overwhelmed the reality of war. On Christmas Eve the British and German soldiers climbed out of their trenches, and for several magical hours, the guns were silent. Enemy soldiers shook hands, looked each other in the eye, exchanged a little whiskey, and shared photos of sweethearts and wives. This peace in the midst of battle is a miracle because it "endures the chaos of life."[69]

Sometimes our feelings of peace are obvious. John and I have vacationed several times at a resort in Mexico, where the employees' greeting is *"Senora, muy tranquilo aqui!"* (Very peaceful here!) Last summer in North Carolina, John commented that I seemed content. *Si, muy tranquilo aqui tambien!* I reflected on my day. The sunrise revealed a crystal clear view of the mountains as I read my Bible on the outside porch, I walked with a friend, baked cookies, played a few holes of golf, napped with Spencer during a late afternoon thunderstorm. Now that is peace I can understand.

Another thing I had done on my "peaceful" day was to write a sympathy note to a couple whose outstanding eighteen-year-old son had been killed in an accident the previous week. If there is peace in that house, it is the "peace . . . which transcends all understanding" (Phil. 4:7), a gift emanating from their faith in Jesus, the one who longs to gather his children together "as a hen gathers her chicks under her wings" (Mt. 23:37). When our peace is deeply rooted in the person of Christ, it is possible to find peace in the midst of tragedy, strife, challenges, and hard times. But be warned, there is an enemy, the thief whose goal is to rob, kill, and steal this peace. The "father of lies" wants us to think that peace cannot exist where there is pain and suffering. This perjurer would want us asking, "Where is God?" when we are hurting. But we know the answer. He is beside, beneath, below, above, and within.

PRAYER

Father, you want us to have peace. When we are tempted to worry, help us to trust you instead. As we seek your face in all the circumstances of this day, we know we will find peace in your presence. And help us to be an instrument of your peace in any relationship that has conflict or misunderstanding.

SCATTERGORIES

*Do not be anxious about anything, but in every situation, by prayer and
petition, with thanksgiving, present your requests to God. And the
peace of God, which transcends all understanding, will guard
your hearts and your minds in Christ Jesus.*

—Philippians 4:6–9

In the game "Scattergories," the players make lists of
things in specified categories: school supplies, American
presidents, dog breeds, items in a refrigerator. All the words
in the list must begin with the same letter, which is established by a roll of the dice. When we recently played the
game with a group of friends, I challenged them with a new
category of my own: words beginning with "p" that describe the "peace that transcends understanding" that Paul
writes about in Philippians. We were all concerned about a
young mother whose husband had died suddenly of a heart
attack, and we wanted to encourage her to find peace in the
midst of grief. We were quite inspired and made a long list.
(Fortunately, we were not working with the letter "q".)

These were some of the words in our list: profess,
providence, Paraclete, paradise, pardon, paschal Lamb,
passion of Christ, pearl of great price, priority, prayer,
praise, purchased, power, preparation, Prince of Peace,
protected, plans, pathway, Presence, proclaim, penitence,

promises, Person, patience, provision, perspective, prophecy, perseverance, purified, Passover.

Over the following weeks, I meditated on these precious words and found that they are the foundation of Jesus' kind of peace that is independent of our circumstances, a peace that can sustain and uphold us. Each of these words could form the basis for prayer and meditation as we ponder the perplexity of pursuing peace, while we are pilgrims on this planet, on the path to Paradise:

The Prophets predicted that
God's plan presented
God's progeny, the Prince of Peace,
His precious provision
For our perpetual protection.
The providential plan of the parent, *Abba*
To offer his Son as the Paschal Lamb.
Peace, the parentheses of his life,
Proclaimed by angels at his birth,
Promised by Jesus before his death,
Prepared for us as a pearl of great price,
Purchased by his blood,
Punished to procure our pardon,
Our penalty paid.

Freed from the prison of poor choices,
The portals of Paradise open,
We pursue our pilgrimage.

Is it our priority to praise him,
Our perspective to seek him?
Pouring out our hearts
In a posture of prayer?
Our place in his presence
Our privilege to profess him.

Does pride prevent us?
Do possessions overly please us?
The perjurer persuades us

That problems preclude
The possibilities that are in
God's power to present us.
Ponder what is pure,
Put on the armor to fight
The power of evil.
Plant yourself by Living Water,
Pursue pathways to righteousness.
The promise is a Person.
We, the people of his pasture
Held safely in the palm of his hand.
We are his possession,
Precious in his sight.
Persevere through the pain,
The Paraclete is beside you,
Be patient as the Potter shapes you.

PRAYER

Lord, how majestic is your name in all the earth. You gave us the gift of language so we could describe you with words. Any letter of the alphabet can open a new way for us to praise you. Listen to these words, one for each letter of the alphabet (except Q and X), and let them be the foundation of our praise. Almighty, Benefactor, Creator, Divine, Everlasting, Father, Gracious, Helper, Infinite, Judge, King, Loving, Majestic, Nurturing, Omnipotent, Provider, Refuge, Shepherd, Teacher, Understanding, Vine, Worthy, Yahweh, Zealous.

```
                    GOD
                    R
                    SAVED
                    C
              SINNER
              A
        LOVE
              I
              O
              REGRET
                    R
                    A
                    C    R
              RENEW
                    S
                    T
                    O         GRACE
                    R         O
              SECOND
                    H
                    A
              TRANSFORMED      R        J
                    C          P        O
        GRACE          ETERNITY
                                  N
                                  T
```

TWENTY-SIX

PRAISE GOD ANYWAY

Sing to the Lord, all the earth; proclaim his salvation day after day.
Declare his glory among the nations, his marvelous deeds among all peoples.
For great is the Lord and most worthy of praise.
—1 Chronicles 16:23–25

In the Psalms, the full range of human emotion is poured out to God—anger, despair, remorse, grief, thanksgiving, hope, and praise. Nothing is held back, no feeling is edited. If you ever feel tongue-tied before the Almighty, this prayer book of the Bible can give wings to the thoughts and emotions of your heart. From psalms of praise to psalms of lament, you can find one to match your mood or circumstance.

It is true that God wants us to express all of our feelings to him in constant communication. But we must also understand that he desires our praise. Praise comes naturally and spontaneously when things are going well—when our relationships are smooth, our children are happy, our lives have meaning and purpose, when we enjoy good health and financial security. Last year, we prayed for two friends who were critically ill. When they both recovered, we said, "God is good, praise God." We would have selected a psalm of thanksgiving or praise.

But sometimes things don't turn out as we had hoped or prayed. When a loved one dies tragically or too young, our hearts are heavy and we may not be in the mood to praise God. Instead, we might gravitate to a psalm of lament. In the midst of this grief, in spite of the circumstance, will we still say, God is good; praise God? Do we eagerly praise God "when the world is all as it should be" but withhold our praise "on the road marked with suffering"?[70]

If we can praise God in the midst of, in spite of, and in the meantime, we will be developing the attitude of PGA (I am not changing the subject to the Professional Golfers Association!). PGA is a choice to Praise God Anyway, even when our hearts are heavy with sadness, when our prayers were not answered. The discipline of PGA in the life of a believer is a powerful evidence of faith. People pay attention when we can praise God "on the road marked with suffering." The Acts of the Apostles provides an example. When Paul and Silas were imprisoned, their legs in the stocks, having been badly beaten, "they were praying and singing hymns of praise to God" (anyway) "and the other prisoners were listening to them" (Acts 16:25). It is very possible they were singing the psalms.

How do we PGA when we don't feel like it? A certain kind of psalm, the psalms of transition, can help us find our way to praise. Although these psalms do culminate in worship and praise, they begin in quite a different way. When we are distressed, anxious, fearful, or hopeless, following the same pattern and progression can help us.

The psalmist begins by pouring out his heart to God, his focus on the problem or circumstance. Everything is expressed—complaint, desire for revenge, self-pity, anger, remorse, bitterness, and bewilderment. God can handle all our emotions! Although he weeps with us, he remains strong. He holds our tears in a bottle, wanting to contain our lament as well as our praise.

Now that the psalmist has limbered up his prayer muscles, a transition is about to begin. The psalmist interrupts his weeping, worrying, and whining with simple words: but, yet, still, again; phrases like "I am still confident of this," "I will yet praise him," "But, this I know." These seemingly insignificant words are powerful, almost holy words signaling that "the minor mode of complaint or penitence" is about to change to the "major key of thanksgiving and praise."[71] But not yet.

The next step in the transition is to remember. The psalmist reflects on past times when he joyfully worshiped God. He remembers God's mighty works, his presence, his power, his deliverance and salvation.

Having poured out his heart, having remembered God's help in the past, the psalmist now looks to the future. He anticipates a time when he will again praise God, a time when the weeping of the night will be eclipsed by morning joy, mourning will turn into dancing, sackcloth will be replaced by the clothing of joy, and his grieving heart will sing a new song to God.

And then we realize that a shift of mood, attitude, or perspective has occurred. Lament has transitioned into praise, sorrow to rejoicing, despair to hope. Someone weeping by the rivers of Babylon suddenly takes up a harp and sings (anyway) even in a foreign land. A person who has felt cast down, disquieted, grief stricken, oppressed, afflicted, scattered, and rejected by God suddenly exclaims, "God is my exceeding joy!" (Ps. 43). PGA! Reading the psalm again, you realize that "even in its most sorrow-laden passages, you feel you are walking in a smoldering volcano of praise, liable to burst out at any moment into a great flame of thanksgiving to God."[72] The skeptic would credit this transition from lament to praise to a change in circumstance, reasoning that the psalm writer's problem or suffering must have been resolved. Life was good again. I think the skeptic might be mistaken. God desires and demands our praise because, as a loving and good Father, he knows that in praising him, his children are blessed.

When we praise God for who he is, our perspective changes. No longer do we need to tell God how big our problem is—we can tell our problem how big God is. Praising him reminds us of his promises, assures us of our value.

As we praise him, we settle into the comfort of knowing how much he loves us. Praise and thanksgiving usher us into his courtyard where the darkness of the world begins to dissipate. Healing and peace are the result because praise "has an element of joy in it."[73]

And a change begins, perhaps not in our immediate circumstance, but in our heart and soul. We can share the experience of the writer of Psalm 46. In the midst of catastrophic circumstances—the earth changing, the mountains quaking, the nations raging, and kingdoms toppling—we can choose to Praise God Anyway—as "refuge, strength, an ever present help in trouble," and the result of praise is to help us hear God say, "Be still and know that I am God." This stillness, this peace, is the result of praise.

PRAYER

Help us, Father, to "turn our eyes upon Jesus, look full in his wonderful face, and the things of earth will grow strangely dim in the light of his glory and grace."[74] Help us to learn the blessing and benefit of praising you even when we don't feel like it. When we praise you as the God who is on our side, who is always near, who walks beside us, we may begin to understand the sufficiency of your grace. As we praise you we might find peace in the words of Julian of Norwich (1416): "all shall be well and all shall be well and all manner of things shall be well", because you have given us yourself, which is enough. "O Lord, open my lips, and my mouth will declare your praise"— anyway!

TWENTY-SEVEN

WAITING

We wait in hope for the Lord; he is our help and our shield.
In him our hearts rejoice, for we trust in his holy name.
—Psalm 33:20–22

Truly my soul finds rest in God...
—Psalm 62:1

Throughout the Psalms, we are exhorted to rest in the Lord and to wait patiently for him. The words *rest* and *wait* seem almost contradictory because, in my experience, they seldom exist simultaneously. Although these words do not exactly fit the definition of an oxymoron (words of opposite meaning being used together) they remind me of words and phrases such as bittersweet, deafening silence, clearly misunderstood, old news, and open secret.

We are waiting for something every day. We wait in the checkout line, for our turn at the gas pump, for our slow high speed internet to log in, for a real person to come on the phone line. This kind of waiting is annoying and frustrating. It is a test of our patience—a fruit of the Holy Spirit—supposedly a virtue of Christians.

Other times our waiting involves matters of great importance: waiting for the results of a CT scan, waiting for the heaviness of grief to abate, waiting for a loved one to return to their faith, waiting for a child to find a job or a spouse. We wait for dreams to be fulfilled, for prayers to be answered. This kind of waiting is a test of our faith and requires that we "be strong and take heart" (Ps. 27:14) as we wait on the Lord.

A new training regimen for our spaniel, Spencer, caused me to reflect again on the challenge of resting while we wait. Having mastered "sit" and "stay," he is now learning a new command: "WAIT." When I leave home with laundry, purse, grocery list, and keys in my hands, Spencer wants to dash out the door ahead of me, desperate not to endure separation from his master. This is annoying to me and dangerous for him, if he were to rush into the street. So Spencer is being trained to "wait." As I close the door leading into the garage to get in my car, he is still sitting, head cocked to the side, waiting.

What does he do while I am gone? What attitude characterizes his time of waiting? Is he restful or restless? Does he waver between trust and doubt, a "double-minded" (Jas. 1:8) dog, one minute relaxing as he confidently awaits my return, the next minute convinced he has been forever abandoned—whimpering, whining, pacing, standing by the door in a lonely, panting vigil? As Spencer's devoted owner, I like to think that he is contentedly curled up in his bed, so confident of my love that he is resting while he waits for me to return.

Resting implies trust, peace, hope, and confidence. We all yearn for true rest of mind, body, and soul, but can we have this attitude as we wait? The writer of the Epistle to the Hebrews warns us not to fall short of "entering his rest" (Heb. 4:1). To enter suggests initiative on our part. Certain attitudes might help us to rest when we face stressful challenges:

> ⬩ Know that God is the only source of true rest.
> ⬩ Give him your concerns and trust that he is working—in his timing.
> ⬩ Cultivate an awareness of his near presence.
> ⬩ Focus on his character.

God Is the Source of True Rest

"Truly my soul finds rest in God." (Ps. 62:1)

At some level, we know that God is the true source and possibility of rest in the midst of our waiting. But the world offers so many alluring and tangible options for rest that we can forget to look to him for peace. Resorts, retirement, and remedies entice us to trust them as a source of rest. Our mattresses and medicine cabinets promise rest; every city block has a day spa. A lodge in Washington State offers a pillow menu to guarantee a good night's rest. Of the nine choices, the only one I didn't order was the pregnancy pillow! But my mind was anxious that night, and sleep eluded me, even surrounded by all these promises of rest.

Give God Your Concerns

"Cast all your anxiety on him because he cares for you."
(1 Pet. 5:7)

Sometimes I am reluctant to give God my concerns—convinced that I can handle things on my own. Other times, I quickly give him my concerns—and just as quickly take them back if things are not accomplished according to my sense of the right time.

The behavior of two flower girls at a wedding gave me a picture of this. Sarah dropped her petals deliberately and carefully as she slowly walked down the aisle. Several times she stopped to pick up a petal and put it back in her basket. Reese, the younger sister, strode down the aisle with great determination, flinging rose petals in the faces of the guests, leaving not one petal remaining in her basket. Are we like Sarah, slow and reluctant to give God our problems and worries, and then picking them up again, putting them back in our basket? I think God might like us to be like Reese—casting our cares on him, putting all our worries in his basket (and leaving them there).

Focus on His Character

"Turn your eyes upon Jesus, look full in his wonderful face, and the things of earth will grow strangely dim in the light of his glory and grace."[75]

Job learned this. After all his questioning, after all the (bad) advice of his friends, Job was reminded of God's power, love, and sovereignty. Job was finally able to trust the one who "held the dust of the earth in a basket" and "weighed the mountains on the scales and the hills in a balance" (Isa. 40:12). We can also rest in the one who "brings out the starry host one by one and calls forth each of them by name"(Isa. 40:26).

In *The Shack,* by William P. Young, the protagonist meets God in person, portrayed as a large, comfy black woman. She says to Mackenzie, a father suffering over the brutal murder of his daughter, "The real underlying flaw in your life, Mackenzie, is that you don't think I am good. If you knew I was good and that everything . . . is covered by my goodness, then while you might not always understand what I am doing, you would trust me."

When grief, fear, anxiety, and worry cause us to feel like "a wave of the sea, blown and tossed by the wind" (Jas. 1:6), we, like Mackenzie, should simply trust in God's goodness. Focusing on the wonderful Names of God—Rock, Fortress, Strong Tower, Shield, Hiding Place, and Shepherd—can soothe and calm our anxious soul.

Cultivate Awareness of His Nearness

"Rejoice in the Lord always. . . . The Lord is near."
(Phil. 4:4)
"Who shall separate us from the love of Christ?"
(Rom. 8:35)
"Whoever dwells in the shelter of the Most High
will rest in the shadow of the Almighty."
(Ps. 91:1)

"Resting in the shadow of the Almighty" is a wonderful way to think of God's nearness. On a trip to New Mexico, I walked with a friend on a moonlit night. In order to walk in each other's shadow, we had to walk close together. God wants us to walk so close to him that we literally share shadows.

Shadows are more distinct on a dark moonlit night than on a bright sunny day. That night in New Mexico, I could see eyelashes and fingernails in my shadow, the details clear and well defined. In the same way, it is often in the dark night of the soul that God's nearness becomes more distinct and well defined.

Unlike Peter Pan, who became separated from his shadow, we cannot get rid of our shadow. Neither can we flee from the inescapable presence of God, who is shadowing us. "If I go up to the heavens, you are there . . . if I rise on the wings of the dawn, if I settle on the far side of the sea, even there . . . your right hand will hold me fast" (Ps. 139:8–10).

Recently, I was anxious and worried about something, certainly not resting as I waited for a situation to be resolved. Perhaps I should practice what I preach, trying out my own suggestions. I acknowledged that I would only find true rest in God. I cast my cares on the one who cares for me—determined to let go and let God. I focused on his character and I imagined him walking by my side. It helped.

But I can become impatient with God's sense of timing. After all, he is the one who says, "a day is like a thousand years, and a thousand years are like a day" (2 Pet. 3:8). Who can deal with that? I want a solution now! Today! Like Spencer, I want to run out the door ahead of him. But this is dangerous. Scripture is replete with stories of people who grew weary with waiting for God to act. Because they were restless as they waited, they took the situation in their own hands, often with disastrous consequences.

Can we accept that although God may accomplish things more slowly than we desire, he is never late? Can we rest in the knowledge that his timing is always the right time? "The Lord is not slow in keeping his promise, as some understand slowness" (2 Pet. 3:9).

Hear his voice: "Come to me, all you who are weary and burdened, and I will give you rest" (Mt. 11:28). Know that God is walking behind you, picking up your worries and concerns and putting them in his basket. "Turn your eyes upon Jesus" and focus more on the person of Christ than on your problem. Imagine that in this dark night of uncertainty you and God are walking side by side, in each other's shadow.

PRAYER

We are all waiting for something. Prayers seem to remain unanswered and we wait, we wait. We wait for something to end, something to begin, something to change. We are in a hurry. We want to add the word now *to our prayer requests. God is answering us:*

- *Now is the time to learn that I am the source of your rest and peace.*
- *Now is the time to cast your cares on me.*
- *Now is the time to focus on my character.*
- *Now is the time to be aware of my nearness.*

TWENTY-EIGHT

TELL ME THE OLD, OLD STORY

Tell me the old, old story of unseen things above,
Of Jesus and his glory, of Jesus and his love.
Tell me the story simply . . . tell me the story slowly . . .
Tell me the story often, tell me the story softly.[76]

The writer of this beloved hymn understood that we should approach much of Scripture as "an immense, sprawling, capacious narrative"[77]—basically a story.

Good literature in the form of a novel or short story portrays characters that engage our imagination and emotions. We identify with their dreams and struggles; we laugh and cry with them and feel a void when we turn the last page. Whether these characters delight you, frustrate you, or disappoint you, they become a part of you. Who can forget Gatsby, Captain Ahab, Holden Caulfield, Scarlett O'Hara, Huck Finn, David Copperfield, or Atticus Finch? When a story has an ambiguous conclusion that leaves us with unresolved questions, we invent our own ideas about what might have happened to a favorite or fascinating character.

A ninety-six-year-old gentleman, Mr. Pennington, is a friend of my ninety-three-year-old mother-in-law. He became obsessed with the fate of the two main characters in my husband's novel *Cardigan Bay*. Charles Davenport and Mary Kennedy fell in love during the tumultuous and uncertain years of World War II. When Charles rejoined his regiment to train for the D-Day landings at Normandy, Mary waited anxiously in her seaside cottage in Ireland. Charles was badly wounded but survived. In the novel's closing scene, Charles, on crutches, enters the back door of the rural Irish church where Mary is praying and worshipping. Even though the novel ends here, most readers are satisfied that this is a "happily ever after" ending. Not true for Mr. Pennington. Because Charles and Mary had walked right off the pages of the novel into his heart, his anxiety for their welfare and happiness was causing him to lose sleep. John wrote Mr. Pennington a letter to assure him that Charles and Mary were doing fine.

Has Jesus become that real to us? Has he walked off the onionskin pages of our Bibles into our hearts so we understand his dreams, struggles, disappointments, and challenges? Or is Jesus asking us the same question he asked Philip? "Don't you know me . . . even after I have been among you such a long time?" (Jn. 14:9). Do we see him as the "brilliant, creative, challenging, fearless, compassionate, [and] unpredictable" man that he was?[78] Or are we people who "know the great truths without feeling the truth of them"?[79]

Eugene Peterson, in *Eat This Book*, says we must pay attention to the form in which Scripture comes to us— mainly as narrative and story. If we miss the form, we will miss much of the content as well. He says that we are often "surprised that Divine revelation arrives in the ordinary garb of story. We think it is our job to dress it up in the latest Paris silk gown of theology, or to outfit it in a sturdy three-piece suit of ethics."[80] We don't take stories seriously because we think they are for children only.

Stories are valuable because they allow us to be participants in the drama. As we combine faith and imagination, we find our place in the story and begin to identify with the characters and feel their emotions.

In *Jesus, the One and Only*, Beth Moore writes that God

approves when we use our imaginations to picture his Son as real. She suggests we "pencil a picture of Christ on the canvas of [your] mind" so that he doesn't remain "faceless and devoid of personality." She writes that we should "avoid imagining Christ as so deep you'd have to dig to find him, or so spiritual his head would be in the clouds. . . . He was a man who could preach an anointed sermon, and then change a flat tire on the way home from church."

If we approach the Gospel of John as a story, we can imagine walking along with Jesus on the dusty roads of Palestine, feeling the sand between our toes, hearing the clacking of palm fronds blown by Middle Eastern breezes, experiencing the thirst caused by the arid desert heat. Standing on the edge of the crowd, we watch his expression change as he interacts with different people. We hear the tone of his voice as he teaches, heals, comforts and confronts.

Movie producers have confused the issue of the real Jesus with their own ideas of what he was like. In the film *King of Kings*, Cecil B. DeMille depicted Jesus as a combination of Ashley Wilkes in *Gone with the Wind* and Mr. Rogers with a beard. In a 1960 film by Pier Paolo Pasolini, an angry (Italian) Jesus strides across the barren landscape uttering terse remarks over his shoulder. In the BBC film *The Son of Man,* Jesus, short and fat with wavy hair, tells the antagonistic religious authorities to "shut up!"

Will the real Jesus please stand up? I want to know him because it will help me to trust him. Trusting him will result in more peace, less anxiety, and less compulsion to plan everything, fix everything, and anticipate everything. We want our experience to be like the one Donald Miller describes in *Blue Like Jazz*: "In the early days, it seemed God was down a dirt road, walking toward me. Years ago, he was a swinging speck in the distance; now he is close enough I can hear his singing. Soon I will see the lines on his face."

In John's Gospel, we observe the development of people's faith through progressive levels of their knowledge of Jesus. The story of the Samaritan woman exemplifies this progression. She knows Jesus first as weary traveler, then

Jew, then Prophet. As she allowed his words to perplex and challenge, she joins her fellow villagers in saying, "This man really is the Savior of the world" (Jn. 4:42).

There is a time-honored way of reading the Scripture known as *lectio divina* (Latin for divine reading) by which our reflections on the words of the Bible inspire our prayers. St. John of the Cross sets forth his thoughts on praying the words of Scripture:

> Seek in READING,
> and you will find in MEDITATION,
> knock in PRAYER
> and it will be open to you in CONTEMPLATION.

Over the period of a week, my reading and meditations on the story of Jesus and the Samaritan woman became the foundation of my prayers. I learned new insights about Jesus and about myself.

Day 1: I praised God as the one who sees no boundary of race, ethnicity, gender, or nationality; the one who sees no line of tradition or custom that he will not cross to save one person.

Day 2: I confessed my meager trust in him. As soon as I request his help, I immediately impose a limitation on his power to act, even doubting at times his willingness to help me. "Sir, the well is deep and you have no bucket." How can I forget that he has all the resources in his mighty hand?

Day 3: I thanked him for his patience as I make slow progress in my journey toward maturity, for his willingness to remain two days with the Samaritan villagers as they sought to understand his identity. I know he is willing to spend time with me in the same way.

Day 4: I prayed that God would increase my sensitivity to the outcasts of our own society, those in our midst who might feel ashamed of their past. For those who feel isolated and unsatisfied, those who may be seeking love in all the wrong ways. I asked God to open my eyes to those who are "ripe for harvest."

Day 5: I prayed that I would look for his presence as I go about the mundane tasks of the day, just as the Samaritan woman encountered Jesus while filling her water jar.

Day 6: I imagined Jesus praying for me to trust him as my source of contentment and significance, seeing potential in me that the world does not recognize. He asks that I not be satisfied with plain water, but to quench my thirst only with his living water.

Day 7: Having spent my entire week in the practice of *lectio divina*—reading, meditating, and praying through this story, I arrived at a point of silent contemplation, which has been described as "a resting in God, a loving gaze upon him, a knowing beyond knowing, a rapt attention to God . . . something that transcends the thinking and reasoning of meditation."[81] And it was here that I felt his near presence, heard him singing, and saw the lines on his face.

PRAYER

Father, we want you to be as real to us as the fictional characters Charles and Mary were to Mr. Pennington. Sometimes we more easily grasp your divinity than we do the reality of your humanity. Sometimes it is easier for us to think of you high and exalted, majestic and mysterious in heaven, than it is to think of you dwelling among us. Two thousand years after you walked and lived on this earth, we have difficulty grasping the reality that you shared our experience and felt our emotions. The creator of the universe was hungry, thirsty, fatigued, discouraged, and disappointed. You wept and laughed. You celebrated and suffered. In order for us to embrace your divinity and humanity in the fullness of each, we must do as the hymn says and continue to hear the story repeated—simply, slowly, often, and softly.

TWENTY-NINE

SEEKING THE FACE OF GOD

> *May God be gracious to us*
> *and bless us and make*
> *his face shine on us.*

—Psalm 67:1

From the moment the first bird tested its wings, the first stars twinkled in the night sky, the first waves crashed against the newly created shore, "The aim of God in history [has been] the creation of an all-inclusive community of loving persons, with Himself included in that community as its prime sustainer and most glorious inhabitant."[82] From the moment God breathed life into Adam, the desire of God's heart has been for us to be in relationships—with each other and with him. God created Eve so that Adam would not be alone. And, to complete the fellowship between husband and wife, God walked in the garden with them in the cool of the day. God has planted in the human heart a desire and need for relationships that are up-close and personal, face-to-face.

We look for the man in the moon, for faces in clouds. We teach our children to shake hands and look people in the eye. When we can't be with someone in person, our technological age provides many ways for us to stay connected through email, text messages, Skype, and Facebook.

When our son Jeff was an infant, I could be persuaded to purchase anything that promised to increase his happiness or intelligence. An image of a face suspended over his crib was supposed to comfort him when he awoke in the night with the assurance that he was not alone. I think it terrified him!

In the movie *Cast Away*, the character portrayed by Tom Hanks is stranded on a desert island after his plane crashes. Isolation from human contact brings him to the brink of madness. Salvation arrived when some cargo washed ashore—a box of volleyballs. After cutting his hand on a shell, his bloody handprint on one of the balls looks remarkably like a human face. Hanks's sanity is restored by his relationship with "Wilson," the ball who becomes his confidant, advisor, and best friend.

In our spiritual life, this yearning for personal and intimate relationship with God is expressed as seeking the face of God. The Old Testament Concordance in my Bible has thirty-five references to "face". God instructed Moses with this priestly benediction: "The Lord bless you and keep you; the Lord make his face shine on you and be gracious to you" (Num. 6:24–25). The manifestations of God's presence in fire, smoke, clouds, and miracles did not quench the yearning to see his face. "My heart says . . . 'Seek his face!'" (Ps. 27:8).

The fulfillment of this longing with the birth of Jesus is well expressed by Simeon: "Sovereign Lord, as you have promised, you may now dismiss your servant in peace. For my eyes have seen your salvation" (Lk. 2:29–30). God, with flesh and bones, had come in human form to walk among us. God showed his face to the world, shook hands, and looked humanity in the eye. The apostle John describes his personal experience with Jesus. "We have seen with our eyes . . . we have looked at and our hands have touched" (1 Jn. 1:1). People walked with him, ate with him, and heard him teach. But this was two thousand years ago and for us the longing remains. We sense that seeing his face is the source of blessing, grace, and peace. Pope Benedict wrote the book *Jesus of Nazareth* because of his desire "to see the face of God."

"For now we see only a reflection as in a mirror; then we shall see face to face" (1 Cor. 13:12). We sing, "Turn your eyes upon Jesus, look full in his wonderful face, and the things of earth will grow strangely dim in the light of his glory and grace."[83] But how? What steps can we take to heighten the reality of his near presence, to brighten our dim vision, to lift the veil that separates us from the Holy One?

A visit to an ancient cathedral in the Sicilian seaside village of Cefalù inspired some thoughts. Stone steps lead up to massive wooden doors. Upon entering, you see the face of Christ on the wall above the altar. Thousands of Byzantine mosaic tiles, created by artisans nearly a thousand years ago, depict a face of strength and tenderness, compassion and sadness. Step by step we walked down the aisle and found a place in the front pew where we silently gazed at the face of Christ.

The photograph I took of the mosaic face of Christ reminds me that the journey of faith is not toward more religion or more spirituality, but toward a person, toward a face. The essence of faith is that God is personal, real, and relational, a God "who in the deep of his mighty nature, thinks, wills, enjoys, feels, loves, desires and suffers as any other person may."[84]

A companion photo is of the stone steps leading to the massive wooden doors of the cathedral, clay pots of pink petunias on the ascending steps. It reminds me that we had to do something that day in Cefalù to see the mosaic face of Christ. We had to make a choice to step away from the charming town square, to step away from the busy marketplace. If we are to see the face of Christ, we must make a similar choice every day—to step away from competing loyalties and distractions and spend time in prayer.

Prayer is the entrance into conversation with our personal, relational God. If anything hinders us from seeing his face, it is failure on our part to enter into this conversation. Just as we had to push through those massive wooden doors to see the mosaic face of Christ, prayer is the way we must "push into sensitive living experience into the Holy Presence, a privilege open to every child of God."[85] Why do we remain outside the Holy of Holies when he is calling us to draw near, "and the years pass and we grow old and tired in the outer courts."[86] Let us not be hindered.

In our rustic church in our small community in North Carolina, the pastor gave a sermon, "The Ladder of Prayer," suggesting a progression of steps that lead us to the waiting presence of God. Many of us are familiar with the pattern of prayer suggested by the acronym ACTS (adoration, confession, thanksgiving, and supplication). Beginning with adoration, the other steps flow naturally. As we praise God for who he is, we see ourselves in his light and recognize the need for confession. Thanksgiving flows from gratitude that we have been forgiven. Then we are ready for personal supplications for others and ourselves. In Pope Benedict's *Jesus of Nazareth*, he suggests a different progression in prayer, that the Lord's Prayer should be prayed backward. In his opinion, we are not ready for the pinnacle of saying "Our Father" until we have taken the steps up the ladder—beginning with supplication, thanksgiving, and confession—finally culminating in adoration and praise.

Perhaps we might try ascending the steps of prayer backward. Beginning with the decision to step away from the distractions of the busy market place:

Place your foot on the first step: Personal petitions. Come boldly before the throne of grace. Present your requests to your loving Father. Give him the worries that cause sleepless nights, the things that make you anxious and rob you of peace. Talk to God about your fears, your dreams, and hopes. Ask him to give you victory over the challenges and temptations you might face this day.

Climb to the second step: Supplication for others. Let God bring to your heart someone who needs your prayers, someone who might be so deeply in pain or suffering that they can no longer pray for themselves.

Place your foot on the third step: Thanksgiving. Remember to "enter his gates with thanksgiving" (Ps. 100:4), with a heart full of gratitude, knowing that it is from "out of his fullness we have all received grace" (Jn. 1:16).

Place both feet firmly on the next step: Confession. Make yourself linger there, even though this is a step you might want to jump over. Spend time with God in honest confession of the sins that block your clear view of his face. Examine what has caused you to stray and wander, know your transgressions, and pray for his forgiveness.

Now, you are ready for the step of Praise and Adoration. "Praise the Lord! How good it is to sing praises to our God, how pleasant and fitting to praise him!" (Ps. 147:1). Because you have stood on all the other steps, your words of praise have been given wings. Praise him for caring about your life, for loving the people for whom you have prayed, praise him as the source of all your blessings, praise him for the mercy that has blotted out your transgressions, for washing you whiter than snow.

Is this the last step on the ladder of prayer? Or is there one more? The visiting minister in North Carolina asked us to close our eyes and imagine that we had entered alone in The Church in the Wildwood[87] and, with the scent of pine and the gentle mountain breeze blowing through the open windows, that we were walking slowly down the aisle toward Jesus who had been waiting for us. This final step of prayer is what we did in the church in Sicily. We sat silently on the front pew gazing at the face of Christ, in a prayer beyond words, not thinking about anything—the *nada* of St. John of the Cross, "a graced state of absorption of God, a loving gaze upon him, a rapt attention to God, a time when we are directly seeking the face of the invisible."

It does not matter in what order we pray to God, but our feet should touch every step on the ladder. God is not concerned whether we ascend or descend the steps of prayer, only that we do pray, that we do enter the conversation by stepping away from competing loyalties, thereby opening the way to see his face.

PRAYER

"Jesus, the very thought of thee, with sweetness fills my breast, but sweeter far thy face to see and in thy Presence rest."[88] Help us, Father, to make the daily choice to leave the busy marketplace, to climb the steps of prayer, so that we will be more aware of your near presence and brighten our dim vision. We know that your door is always open as you wait to welcome us. With each step deeper into prayer, our heart opens to yours.*

THIRTY

A SPANIEL'S FALL
FROM GRACE

*No temptation has overtaken you except what is
common to mankind. And God is faithful;
he will not let you be tempted beyond what you can bear.*
—1 Corinthians 10:13

Short, dark, and handsome, Spencer came into our lives a few years ago. We had held this Cavalier King Charles puppy in the palm of our hands when he was two weeks old. When he was five weeks old, we chose him from his littermates, knowing he had to be ours.

As we eagerly awaited the day when Spencer could come home with us, nothing was spared as we planned and prepared an environment to assure his safety and happiness. The provision for his wants and his needs was complete—the specialty food, a plush bed, and an attractive kennel. I even sacrificed my favorite baby pillow. And toys of every kind: cuddly, squeaky, rawhide, and balls.

Eyebrows and cheeks of rust punctuate Spencer's beautiful black-and-white face. The intense gaze of his black eyes expresses so much love that your heart melts. But, as our mothers used to say, "Pretty is, as pretty does." Spencer is a sinner!

Spencer had to live with only one prohibition: "Thou shalt not chew on my mother's needlepoint rug!" He was allowed to chew on other things—pecans, twigs, even my socks! Considering our abundant provision, we expected obedience to this one command. We were disappointed.

John enjoys walking with Spencer in the cool of the day. Arriving home from the office one evening, he couldn't find his puppy. "Where are you, Spencer?" He was hiding under the dining room table, tail between his legs, a look of shame and fear on his face. "What is it that you have done?" This question was answered when we noticed the frayed corner of my mother's rug, puppy teeth marks on the fine stitches. Spencer had seen that the rug was good for chewing and a delight to the eyes. He had not heeded the advice on our cross-stitch pillow: "If sinners entice thee, consent thou not." The consequence for his transgression? He was sent forth from the fellowship and companionship of the family room.

We surmised that Spencer had been deceived by the enemy—the one whose crafty tactics have not changed since the Garden of Eden, tactics that have been practiced and perfected upon vulnerable people (and animals).

- Satan twists the truth. "Spencer, you poor dog, did they say, 'You shall not chew on anything in the house?' Did they say you couldn't even walk on the rug?"
- Satan makes us doubt the goodness of our Master. "They are so strict! They care more about their material possessions than they care about your pleasure and happiness."
- Satan helps us justify our sin. "Puppies who are teething need to chew on something. The fibers in the rug are good for your digestion."
- Satan encourages us to blame others. "What about that other dog, the one whom they gave you so you would not be alone? It was her idea, wasn't it?"
- Satan delights when we involve others in our sin. "Spencer, you should share this pleasure with your

friends." The next day we walked into the family room and saw a veritable feast taking place around my mother's rug. Cat, rabbit, bird, and two dogs nibbling to their hearts' content.

Because this unsuspecting and vulnerable dog had succumbed to the tempter's tactics, Spencer had failed. So do we. Spencer's transgression had the result that sin always has—broken fellowship and separation from the Master. We missed Spencer and wanted to restore the relationship that had been broken by sin. In the end, love covered over a multitude of sins (1 Pet. 4:8), and Spencer was retrieved from his place of exile. We held him in our arms and encouraged him to be a better dog, content with the blessings surrounding him, grateful for our provision. What had caused this dog to fall from grace?

Before The Fall, Adam and Eve had walked with God. Perhaps a careful observation of Spencer's behavior on our walks would help me understand the origin of his disobedience. As his master, the Alpha of his pack, our walks provide me an opportunity for training. It is my responsibility to lead, teach, guide, protect, nurture, and encourage. He needs to understand my expectations and learn to accept boundaries. He will not be allowed to roam at will, but must learn to follow. In learning to heel, he will develop the habit of walking beside me on a loose leash, perfectly synchronized with my speed. As the leader, I determine our route, our pace, and our destination. The many distractions of the street make it difficult for him to hear my voice as I encourage and warn: "Good dog." "Car coming." "Stay by me." "Leave it" when he is tempted by forbidden fruit. Frog jerky is his favorite, but it is unclean and might make him sick. When the walk is long and the day is hot, and the puppy gets weary, I pick him up and carry him home.

Is it possible that canines and humans have something in common in their relationship to their Master? Perhaps the source of Spencer's and our disobedience derives from similar tendencies. As we walk with God, we resist training, strain at the leash, chafe at boundaries. We would like to be the Alpha, the leader of the pack, the one who plans the route and determines the pace, preferring that the Master follow us. We are easily distracted and tempted by things that are not good for us, unclean things that can sicken our souls. How often is God saying, "Leave it"?

Our desire for independence causes us to wander from the intimacy God desires. When the Master's stride seems too slow, we run ahead. Out of range of his voice, we are more vulnerable to the voice of the Tempter.

If Spencer were to run away and get lost, would I be angry? No, I would be frantic and heartbroken, searching the neighborhood, calling his name, posting his picture on every telephone pole. Are there utility poles in heaven? "Lost child, reward if found."

"Prone to wander, Lord, I feel it, prone to leave the God I love."

PRAYER

*W*e should join Spencer in singing these words from a hymn, "Take away the love of sinning; Alpha and Omega be." [89] *Father, we confess our lack of gratitude for your abundant provision. How easily we are tempted to doubt your goodness, blame others, and justify our sin. Help us be alert for Satan's tactics and see the way you have provided for us to fight temptation. Thank you that your steadfast love meets us in our failure and brings us back to fellowship.*

THIRTY-ONE

THE QUILTS OF GEE'S BEND

Gather the pieces that are left over.
Let nothing be wasted.

—John 6:12

     In 2010, I traveled to Atlanta and visited a special exhibit at the High Museum of Art, "The Quilts of Gee's Bend." After walking through several rooms I was disappointed and unimpressed by these utilitarian and plain quilts, which seemed to lack a clear sense of design and pattern. Had I missed part of the exhibit? Perhaps I had overlooked the rooms containing the beautiful quilts, the ones of true artistry.

     Back in the hotel room, I turned to my Bible study for the following week, the story of Joseph in the book of Genesis. As I read about Joseph as a slave in Egypt, I thought about the quilts, created by descendants of former slaves in Alabama who live in a tiny settlement called Gee's Bend. Joseph had his coat of many colors and the "Benders" had their quilts of many colors. What else might they have in common?

     The following day I returned to the museum for a more leisurely visit, curious to see why this exhibit had been so highly recommended. As I strolled the galleries and read the printed information by each quilt, I began to notice the stories—stories of individuals, families, and a community descended from former slaves who had remained at Gee's Bend after the Civil War. Located at a wide curve of the Alabama River, isolated and cut off from any modernity or commerce and accessible only by ferryboat, these people were identified during the Depression as the poorest of America's poor.

With limited choices in life as well as limited choices of materials for their quilts, these women made adjustments and used available resources—old blue jeans, worn work shirts, faded bandannas, and grain sacks. Items we would discard as useless trash, they sewed into quilts to keep their families warm. I began to recognize the true artistry and beauty as each quilt told its unique story.

One of the quilters, Mary Lee Bendolph, was interviewed by J. R. Moehringer for an article in the *Los Angeles Times* (August 22, 1999). Mr. Moehringer won the Pulitzer Prize for feature writing in 2000 for this work. Mary Lee started quilting when she became pregnant in the sixth grade and had to drop out of school. At the time of the article, she was a "round woman with a giggle like one of the river songbirds and a speaking voice pitched between a lullaby and a prayer." As we read her words, we can be inspired by what helped her deal with hardship, privation, and sorrow.

* Mary Lee maintained her compassion for others. She refused surgery because she worried "how my lovely people would survive if left to fend for themselves."
* Mary Lee knew the importance of staying busy in useful occupation. She plans "to keep on moving, doing her chores and seeing to the needs of her lovely people."
* Mary Lee learned patience as she waited for God's timing. "Every Bender knows how to wait. Living here, you learn that fate is like a ferry. It comes when it comes."

- Mary Lee continued to pray and depend on God to help her. "Some people have a good life. But, I had a rough life. But, I thank God that he helped me come through." Like most of the Benders, Mary Lee had a special praying place, a spot to meet and talk to God.
- Mary Lee accepted her circumstances with a sense of humor and without complaining or grumbling. "I'm not a person to be angry. When you be pleasant, your light shine better." She said that she could still laugh in spite of the confusion around her.

These same themes were a part of Joseph's life as he dealt with hardship and bewildering circumstances. He was compassionate to fellow prisoners, noticing their troubled and downcast faces (Gen. 40:6–7). He stayed busy caring for all the other prisoners—having been made responsible for all that was done there (Gen. 39:22). He depended on the Lord's presence and steadfast love (Gen. 39:21). And most amazingly, he was not bitter or angry with his brothers, who had sold him into slavery, understanding that God had been in control, that "it was to save lives that God sent me ahead of you" (Gen. 45:5). Joseph's attitude is best revealed in the names he gave his children: Manasseh, "God has made me forget all my trouble," and Ephraim, "God has made me fruitful in the land of my suffering" (Gen. 41:52).

Had proximity to a river taught them something? Joseph near the Nile, the Benders by the Alabama River? There is a quote etched in a wall by the San Antonio River, as if the river itself is speaking: "Like life, *como la vida*, I have made adjustments, bending here and there, *continuamente* [continuously]."

Making adjustments and bending here and there reflects the quality of resilience, a stronger and more positive word than endurance. Mary Lee and Joseph were both resilient as they suffered privation and mistreatment. Their attitude of keep-on-keeping-on as they made adjustments to circumstances kept them from bitterness and anger. Rick

Warren suggests a resilient person accepts that life is not an alternating series of good and bad, but is more like parallel railroad tracks—the presence of good and bad, lemons and lemonade at the same time.

Resilience bore fruit in the lives of Mary Lee and Joseph. Because the future was not constrained or tainted by bitterness and anger, they both experienced an outcome beyond their dreams and expectations. As Joseph languished in prison, falsely accused by Potiphar's wife, he would never have imagined his future position of prominence in Egypt that resulted in saving God's chosen people from famine. The quilters of Gee's Bend would never have imagined that their utilitarian quilts would be displayed in one of the finest art museums in the country, touted as "genius emerging from want."[90]

Making a quilt is a labor of love and time. Let's use our sanctified imagination. God has invited you to a quilting bee where together you will create a patchwork quilt that will tell your life story.

In a basket are the patches, each one representing a season, an event, circumstance, relationship, or a turning point in your life. Wanting to make an attractive quilt that is neat and tidy, you carefully select the patches to incorporate. You prefer ones that represent times of happiness, peace, health, prosperity, and good relationships. Your fingers are nimble and the memories are pleasant as you stitch these into your quilt. But there are other patches that are frayed, tattered, and faded. You would like to ignore or even throw them away because they remind you of pain, grief, suffering, broken relationships, illness, and death. We didn't want these things when they were a part of life. Why would we choose them for our quilts?

As you toss them aside, God picks them up and tells you that these need to be a part of your quilt because they are part of your story. Have you forgotten the lessons of the quilters of Gee's Bend? Nothing is wasted. Nothing is useless. Remember that Mary Lee pronounced "Gee's Bend" as "Jesus Been." If you include these in your quilt, you will remember times when you were resilient, times when you made adjustments, and you will remember that "Jesus Been" there for all those times, continuamente.

And, with his own hands, he stitches the patches into your quilt. It may not be as pretty or as neat and tidy as you wanted, but it will be beautiful because it tells the story of a life, a family, and a community. Yours! And mine! Your quilt will not hang in the High Museum of Art in Atlanta, but in the rooms of the Highest Heaven. And the angels will walk by and comment, "fearfully and wonderfully made." Your life!

PRAYER

Father, help us learn the wisdom of Joseph and Mary Lee in the face of hardship and suffering. To remain compassionate, stay busy, be patient, keep praying, maintain a sense of humor, and refrain from complaining. And most of all to always find a praying place to be with you. We are eager to collect and remember good and happy times, but we know that "Jesus Been" with us through all times. And we will accept that no experience is wasted or useless.

THIRTY-TWO

GOD'S WALKING PARTNER

*Surely everyone goes around like a mere phantom; in vain they rush about,
heaping up wealth without knowing whose it will finally be.*
—Psalm 39:6

*I cannot think of a single advantage I've ever gained
from being in a hurry.*[91]
—Ann Voskamp

The Hebrew word *Halakah* refers to the way a person should walk before God in his or her daily life. The Old Testament has only three references to people who actually walked with God: Enoch, Noah, and Adam and Eve before Satan slithered onto the scene. This concept of walking with God continues in the New Testament as we are told to "walk in obedience to his commands" (2 Jn. 1:6) and to walk in the truth. In popular terms, we are supposed to walk the walk, not just talk the talk.

Since God desires to be in a relationship with his people, he is looking for walking partners. What might characterize our spiritual walk with God? Belief, obedience, sharing, intimacy, delight, and dialogue. Philip Yancy calls it "keeping company with God." Does this describe your walk with God?

Is it possible that the manner in which we walk physically might reveal something about our spiritual walk?

A week in Paris gave me the opportunity to observe cultural differences between French and American walkers—differences in pace, attitude, demeanor, and purpose.

The French are not in a hurry, even in a busy city like Paris. A chic, refined, mañana attitude characterizes their walking. Parents taking their children to school lean over the stone bridge to watch ducks float by on the River Seine below. They stop to admire the changing autumn leaves. In the afternoon, the family strolls at an even slower pace as they enjoy pastries or ice cream cones.

The dictionary defines vacation as "freedom from duty, business, or activity; becoming unoccupied." Even though my husband and I were on vacation, we Americans still seemed to be in a hurry. Delays, detours, and interruptions were not welcome. We had things to accomplish! In the morning, we hurried to the neighborhood boulangerie to get the freshest croissant. After lunch, we hurried to Berthillon, the famous ice cream shop on the Ile St. Louis, to avoid the long lines. And then we waited *impatiently*—as the French leisurely selected their favorite flavors among ninety-nine choices. In the late afternoon, we hurried to reach St. Chappelle before it closed. Whew!

In Frank Lloyd Wright's *An Autobiography* he mentions that when he was nine years old, his uncle, James Lloyd Jones, advised him to walk the American way. Concerned about Frank's wandering path, he told the boy to walk in a straight line, never deviate from his goal, and never waste time. Frank decided on a different philosophy of life. He knew if he walked the way his uncle advised, he would miss the most beautiful and important things in life. Frank learned the value of wandering and meandering.

A guide we engaged for a walking tour of 1920s Paris demonstrated the French attitude. After making slow progress through the Montparnasse neighborhood, he stopped outside the Luxembourg Gardens to reminisce about his daughter, Louise, who used to ride ponies there. He then drew our attention to the pattern of fallen chestnut leaves on the wet pavement! He sensed my impatience when I glanced at my watch and then he said something that this American needed to hear and remember: "Sometimes the best walk is standing still." My "hurry up, you move too slow" was answered by his "slow down, you move too fast."

The French saunter for pleasure. We Americans stride with purpose. Henry David Thoreau understood the difference: "There is an art to walking, but we must develop a genius for sauntering."[92]

The word *saunter* derives from the Middle Ages when pilgrims on their way to the Holy Land were said to be going *á la saint terre*, "to the Holy Land." In time they were called "Holy Landers" or "Saint terrers." You can hear how the word *saunter* came about. I think God would prefer a French walking partner. Their walking is about relationships, communication, connection, intimacy, and interaction. Less about destination and more about the journey. Less about a purpose and more about enjoying the company of their walking partner.

If God is our walking partner, are we enjoying him as stated in the Westminster Catechism? "The chief end of man is to love God and enjoy him forever." Enjoy God, the catechism says. Our walk with God can become almost legalistic, full of purpose, plans, objectives, and goals, but without pleasure. We got our Schnauzer, Bridget, when she was a year old. Her previous owners had trained her well, in hopes she would be a show dog. As I walked with her, her flawless obedience was evident. Just as evident was the absence of enjoyment. Bridget was suffering from legalism!

My daily exercise goal is 10,000 steps on a pedometer. I clip the little device to my pajamas when I get up in the morning so those 39 steps to the bathroom get recorded. I want all these steps to count! At the end of the day, I evaluate my walk. Did I walk far enough, fast enough? Did I burn enough calories? Did I increase my heart rate? Would I choose this route again or were there too many detours?

God doesn't want us to waste the steps of our day either. He also wants our walking to count for something. But he may evaluate our walking in a slightly different way, asking us these questions:

- Did those 10,000 steps refresh your soul?
- Did you know that the detour was my best path for you to follow today?
- Did your heart beat faster for anyone with the accelerated beat of compassion and kindness?
- Did you notice I was your constant walking partner?
- Did you stop to notice the loveliness of this world, your dwelling place and mine?

Parents sometimes take their baby's first shoes and have them bronzed. Placed on a tabletop or mantel, they are reminders of a baby's first steps. God formed tiny feet when he "knit [us] together in [our] mother's womb" (Ps. 139:13). He saw us take our first tentative steps toward the outstretched arms of a parent. He saw us take our first baby steps toward belief and faith. The rooms in God's mansion must be overflowing with bronzed baby shoes. And he will be there as we take our final step over the threshold of this life into eternal life into the waiting arms of the Father.

PRAYER

Father, we don't want to be like the men walking along the road to Emmaus. Though Jesus walked with them, they didn't recognize him because of their preoccupation with the events of the day. Help us to be attentive to your presence at our side. We want to walk through this life with you, careful not to rush ahead of your purposes, nor lag behind your will. Help us to allow you to determine the pace, route, and destination of our daily walk. We want to keep company with you in all the steps of our day—loving you, enjoying you, letting you show us "the path of life" (Ps. 16:11). At times we will stumble, at other times veer from your path, but we know you hold us by the hand—leading and guiding all the way.

THIRTY-THREE

LISTENING FOR GOD

To him who rides across the highest heavens,
the ancient heavens, who thunders with mighty voice.
—Psalm 68:33

Today, if you hear his voice, do not harden your hearts.
—Hebrews 4:7

Prayer has been described as an ongoing conversation with God, a two-way communication where both parties talk and listen. C. S. Lewis, before he was a believer, was skeptical about the concept of communicating with God, considering prayer to be a pointless exercise, like sending a letter over and over to someone whose address you are not sure of. Since there is no one to receive the letter, no one will write back. Dallas Willard writes, "Hearing God is a daring idea, some would say presumptuous and even dangerous." But, he continues, "What if we are made for it? What if the human system simply will not function properly without it . . . because we are created for intimate friendship with himself."[93] I feel sure C. S. Lewis discovered that God does write back. But if we are hard of hearing when it comes to his voice, we have failed to open the letter and "hear" his reply.

Perhaps we need to improve our listening skills. We

are so much better at the talking part of our prayer conversation that we tend to keep the conversation one-sided, delivering our monologue to God and not giving him a chance to get a word in edgewise. We have experienced this as parents. Our children call to vent their emotions and then hang up, "Gotta go," before we have been able to give them our wise and compassionate counsel. God has the same experience with his children. We call on his direct line: "Then you will call on me and come and pray to me, and I will listen to you" (Jer. 29:12). We vent our feelings, frustrations, and emotions, and then we hang up, "Gotta go," before God has been able to speak his words of comfort, wisdom, and encouragement. Can we become better conversationalists, better at listening to what God is communicating?

We need to begin with the expectation that God does speak to us. "The mighty one, God, the Lord, speaks and summons the earth from the rising of the sun to where it sets. . . . Our God . . . will not be silent" (Ps. 50:1, 3). There are many voices that clamor for our attention in a noisy world. His is one of them. Like young Samuel, we may need help discerning God's voice. God speaks to young and old. He speaks night and day. He speaks in many ways—through his Word, through other people, through circumstances, through dreams, through nature, and through the indwelling Holy Spirit.

On a trip to Switzerland, I gained some insights about listening. We noticed a continuous tinkling, as if there were wind chimes on every tree in the forest. After a few days in this bucolic country, we discovered the source of the melodious sound. Swiss farmers have used bells on their cows for centuries, primarily to locate the herd in the open alpine meadow. As the animal moves while grazing, the bells ring. The cause of this pleasant ringing was obvious when we saw the cows walking in the middle of the road, on their way to a new pasture. Hiking one day, with no animal in sight, we could still hear the faint tinkling of the bells. It was because we were listening for them. Because we expected that the sound was always present and because we took the time to pause. In the stillness and silence, and with expectation, we could hear those distinctive bells any time, day or night. Do we fail to hear God because we lack the expectation that he is speaking? Do we fail to hear him because we don't pause long enough to give him the gift of our silence?

Selah is a word that appears seventy-one times in the Psalms, usually at a break between passages. Since the Psalms were sung, *selah* in musical terms indicated a pause, an interlude, perhaps signaling a change in melody or rhythm. This interruption in the singing also offered the rabbi an opportunity to speak words of reflection or encouragement. In over thirty years of reading the Psalms, I had not noticed this word, and suddenly I saw it everywhere. There is a Christian music group named Selah and a Texas environmentalist whose ranch is named Selah. A young couple named their baby girl Selah, meaning "pause," "slow down," or "take a breath." Does hearing God's voice require some *selah* in our day, an attitude of pausing to listen?

Lloyd John Ogilvie's relationship with God was deepened when he read a secular book about conversation, which stressed the importance of silent listening. After incorporating these ideas into his prayer life, Ogilvie wrote *Conversations with God* in which he suggests nine steps in our prayer conversation with God. One of these steps, probably the most challenging for us, is silence.

For one week, I added the step of silence to my prayer time, curious to see if it would enhance my conversation with God. I resolved to spend five minutes (Ogilvie suggests ten) with this step of creative solitude and to keep a journal of my experience. Following Ogilvie's suggestion, I sat with my hands open in my lap, in an attitude of receiving, with the expectation of hearing and listening for God's voice. *Selah.*

DAY 1: As I tried to quiet my mind, I identified with the words of the author of *Eat, Pray, Love* as she tried to meditate. She felt "burdened with what the Buddhists call the 'monkey mind'—the thoughts that swing from limb to limb, stopping only to scratch themselves, spit and howl. From the distant past to the unknowable future, [her] mind [swung] wildly through time, touching on dozens of ideas a minute, unharnessed and undisciplined."[94] Settling into the silence seemed impossible. God's voice could not have gotten through to me. I tried hard. I looked at my photo of the Swiss cows with their bells to encourage my listening. I repeated *selah and* I kept peeking at my watch. How could five minutes be so long? I said to my thoughts, "Go outside and play now . . . Mommy's listening to God."[95] No use.

DAY 2: Let's try again. Praise, confession, and thanksgiving went smoothly. Oh no! Time for the step of silent listening. I have waited too long. The phone rings, the dogs are hungry and ready for a walk. The daily distractions have begun, so much to do! The tyranny of the urgent takes over. Cow bells, *selah*. Nothing works. I am a failure at silence.

DAY 3: Because of the frustrating experience of the past two days, I skipped the silence part of my conversation with God and took our dog, Spencer, on a walk in Brackenridge Park. Stopping to rest at a bench under a cypress tree near the flowing water, I decided to try my silent time in this unlikely place. There were no people around, so with Spencer's leash in my hand, I opened my palms in the attitude of receiving for at least five minutes. I can't say that I heard God, but I was more comfortable with the silence, actually feeling serene and relaxed. Was God teaching me that I don't need to be regimented about the time or place of prayer?

DAY 4: Slightly encouraged, I thought this was the day to get really serious about this "silent" time. Since God seemed pretty silent himself, I decided to help the conversation along. My prayer agenda was to talk to God about my daughter who was living in London. As I stilled my thoughts, God changed the focus of my prayer to some issues I needed to confront in my own life. Apparently God thought I was the one who needed some guidance today, not my daughter. Is God teaching me to leave this silent time in his hands, to let him guide me with his agenda?

DAY 5: Back at the bench in Brackenridge Park. Palms up, mind clear, *selah*. Today, God brought to my mind a friend I have not seen for a long time, Mary, my college roommate, with whom I have had only sporadic contact during the past forty years. Since God had spoken her name to me, I prayed for her, having no idea of her current circumstances. Should I have been so amazed when I had a call from Mary a few days later saying she was coming to San Antonio on a business trip?

DAY 6: In my silent time today, God gave me clarity and perspective about some family relationships. Anger gave way to compassion and understanding.

My journey of silence was challenging, awkward, and uncomfortable. It began with frustration, even boredom. I agreed with George Bernard Shaw who "believes in the discipline of silence; he could talk about it for hours!" However, in this week I learned that my silence is a gift to the one who is not silent, and that we need to allow God "to hatch his ideas in our thinking,"[96] to give us the best and wisest prayer for others and for ourselves.

Just as the sound of the bells is always discernible in Switzerland, so is God's voice if we have ears to hear, our ability enhanced by training, practice, and discipline. A pianist, a house-guest who was practicing in our living room, modeled this listening skill for me. As he was forcefully and energetically (and loudly) executing a Chopin prelude, our small Schnauzer entered the room. The young man stopped playing, distracted by the sound of the dog's tags, a sound I had not even noticed. Oh, that we would be so attuned to God's voice as it enters our daily pursuits.

We want to develop Samuel's attitude: "Speak, for your servant is listening" (1 Sam. 3:10). Would a

song about your typical day include the word *selah*—
indicating that you had paused, slowed down, and taken
a breath so that the Rabbi Jesus could interrupt you with
his words of love, encouragement, and comfort? Or did you
hang up too soon? How many of God's words don't reach
us, thus falling to the ground because we have not created those silent times in which to receive them with open
hands, open ears, and an open heart?

So, as you keep company with God in prayerful conversation, try your own journey of silence. Listen for the bells.
Good luck. *Selah*.

PRAYER

*Father, help us to give you silent times to hear your
voice. Help us discern your voice from the many
others that claim our attention and time. And, most of all,
when we do hear you, give us responsive hearts to follow
your guidance, to obey the promptings of your Spirit.*

THIRTY-FOUR

HALLWAYS OF THE BUCKINGHAM: LESSONS FROM A RETIREMENT HOME

I am the gate for the sheep . . .
whoever enters through me will be saved.

—John 10:7, 9

Knock and the door will be opened to you.

—Matthew 7:7

I stand at the door and knock.
If anyone hears my voice and opens the door,
I will come in and eat with that person, and they with me.

—Revelation 3:20

My ninety-three-year-old mother-in-law lives at a retirement home named the Buckingham. She chose the apartment that is farthest from the dining room, reasoning that she would be forced to get more exercise walking to and from meals. To reach her apartment from the main entrance, you walk down several very long hallways, with doors on both sides. An enormous apartment complex for seniors.

Outside each apartment is a small shelf, which the residents decorate with a variety of objects. On one interminable journey down the hallways to her unit, I began to notice the adornments on the shelves outside the doors. There were many crosses, angels, flowers, stuffed animals, figurines, American flags, an oriental plate, a Mexican doll, a Texas A & M baseball cap, a bowl of candy, a life-size statue of a Labrador retriever, and a NASA space ship (not full size).

Knowing that these objects must reveal something about the strangers behind closed doors, I began to make guesses and judgments and invent stories. Many are Christian and most are patriotic. One had traveled to China, another to Mexico, and one had taken the grandkids to Disney World. One is an Aggie, another loves dogs, and one might be retired from NASA. Even if I had peered through their mail slot, my knowledge of this person would still be limited. And if a peephole were on my side of their door, it would give a distorted vision of what is inside. My judgments could be wrong. There is so much more to know about them. Strangers they remain.

Perhaps on my next walk down this hallway, I will encounter an open door with a hand extended in greeting, an invitation to enter the apartment. We would become acquainted as we shared our life stories—career, family, hobbies, travels, and favorite pets. It would be the beginning of relationship. Strangers no longer.

As God's chosen people walked the long corridors of centuries, God revealed himself in many ways. But, with a longing to have more knowledge of their God, they might have used their imagination, making guesses and judgments. There were adornments on the shelf, visible objects that confirmed God's presence and involvement in their lives—a burning bush, pillar of fire, a cloud, and manna from heaven. They witnessed acts and miracles accomplished by the "mighty hand" of the Lord (Exod. 13:14). And because "God will not be silent," God had spoken—sometimes in a voice so loud it would "break the cedars of Lebanon," sometimes in a whirlwind or a whisper, and once through a donkey. Therefore, God's door was not completely shut. But what they could know and see of him was limited, like looking through the mail slot, and perhaps distorted like the view through a peephole. Their longing was deep.

In Psalm 27, David writes, "One thing I asked of the Lord . . . to live in the house of the Lord all the days of my life . . . to behold the beauty of the Lord. Your face, Lord, do I seek." But no one could see God's face and live. The last book of the Old Testament says that God will "throw open the floodgates of heaven and pour out so much blessing that there will not be room enough to store it" (Mal. 3:10). For four hundred years more they waited.

When the "Word became flesh and made his dwelling among us" (Jn. 1:14), God showed his face to the world. Jesus, who "was with God, and . . . was God" (Jn. 1:1), "the radiance of God's glory and the exact representation of his being" (Heb. 1:3), was the full and complete revelation of God. The doors and windows to God's dwelling place were opened wide. No more mail slot, no more peephole. The hand of God was extended in greeting and welcome. Jesus' invitation to "come and see" is for all of us. Come and spend some time with me. Come and live with me, abide with me. I want to hear about your life story—your family, your career, your travels, your hobbies, and favorite pets. What has begun is a relationship, a friendship with the Lord (Ps. 25:14). Strangers no longer.

God has done his part. Have we? As Jesus has walked the long corridors of centuries, he has encountered many closed doors. Revelation 3:20 depicts Jesus standing at a door knocking. Do we keep the safety chain in place and open the door only a crack, suspicious of who is standing outside? Do we feel we have to tidy up our lives before we let him in? Perhaps we are content with a superficial relationship and will only let him know us by the knick-knacks we place on the shelf. Why don't we open the door wide, extend a hand of welcome, and invite him into our lives and our hearts? A word of warning: Jesus is a visitor who has come to stay!

PRAYER

Father, let us never lose the wonder of knowing that in Jesus Christ the door is always open. Your hand is always extended in welcome and invitation. Long before any of us walked a hallway called faith or religion, you had opened your door and were waiting for us to come in. Let us open our hearts to you and not be content to be superficial with a God who already knows us totally. "Friendship with the Lord" (Ps. 25:14) is our gift and privilege if we accept the invitation. A relationship can begin. Strangers no longer.

THIRTY-FIVE

THE KALEIDOSCOPE

There is no shadow of turning with Thee.
Thou changest not,
Thy compassions they fail not.
As Thou has been, Thou forever wilt be.
—Thomas Chisholm

When you peer through the lens of a kaleidoscope, you feel you have stepped inside a cathedral with a beautiful rose window. Designs are created by bits of glass, plastic, and mirror that tumble apart and rearrange themselves into new patterns as you rotate the cylinder. Some of the pieces are bright, others dark, some have smooth edges and regular shapes, others are jagged and irregular. The individual pieces are unremarkable. It is only as they are held together in the cylinder that they become a symbol of potential and possibility. When a turn of the kaleidoscope creates a particularly beautiful pattern, you wish you could hold onto it, returning in an hour, a day, or a month to find that everything was the same. But you cannot reverse the motion and recapture the exact design again. The beauty and fascination of the kaleidoscope is the change that creates new designs.

Throughout the Bible, we see people confronted with

the challenge of change. A repeated theme is that old things pass away to be replaced by the new (2 Cor. 5:17), whether it is the nation of Israel or individual lives. Accepting change requires courage and the confident trust that God has his hand on the process and the outcome. Sometimes change is subtle and slow; sometimes it is sudden and seismic.

With misguided religious zeal, Paul was on his way to persecute and arrest the believers. Before the dramatic encounter with Christ on the road to Damascus, Paul's life had a pattern of which he was proud, confident, and content. The design and shape was familiar and predictable, bound in centuries of custom and tradition from which he derived his purpose and identity. Paul was not expecting things to change. He wanted this pattern to be repeated the next hour, the next day, for the rest of his life. He had confidence in his education, position and the status of Roman citizenship. As a Hebrew, Paul was a member of the people of Israel, from the tribe of Benjamin—a Hebrew born of Hebrews. As a Pharisee, he could boast of righteousness in his faultless observance of the law. Paul would soon evaluate his life differently (Phil. 3:5-6).

When "a light from heaven flashed around him" and he heard Jesus' voice (Acts 9:3–4), the perfectly orchestrated design of Paul's life began to break apart. The pieces of his life that he had cherished, he now considered rubbish (Phil. 3:8). He knew he could not go back to his former way of life, but the future was unclear. In his three days of blindness, Paul must have wondered if he would ever serve God again, ever again feel he was an instrument of the Almighty. As he looked for a reason to hope, he clung to his belief in a God in whom "all things hold together" (Col. 1:17), a God who could contain the broken pieces of his life and transform them into a new pattern.

Let's use our imagination. As a child, Paul had spent most of his time in his father's tentmaker-shop, but he had loved being in the company of the old potter, watching the skilled fingers turn the wheel to shape a formless mass of clay into something both beautiful and useful. One day, Paul watched in horror as a clay vessel of elegant design fell to the floor and shattered. Rubbish, no longer valuable or useful, he thought. Paul was surprised to see that instead of sweeping up the pieces and throwing them in the trash bin, the old man got on his hands and knees and gently gathered the pieces of broken pottery. Immediately, the potter began to apply his creative skill to repair the vessel, never removing his hand in the process.[97]

When Paul wrote that, "we have this treasure in jars of clay" (2 Cor. 4:7), referring to our knowledge of God, he recognized that we are fragile and vulnerable and can be easily broken. When our hopes and dreams are shattered, can we be mended?

I never liked this nursery rhyme: "Humpty Dumpty sat on a wall, Humpty Dumpty had a great fall. All the king's horses and all the king's men couldn't put Humpty together again." It seemed that poor, broken Humpty was beyond hope. On the contrary, when we are broken we know that our King can put the pieces together again. Valuable possessions frequently get broken in our house. I take them to a shop, "Treasured Possessions," in the hope they can be restored. The man who owns the shop once told me that my treasure was not worth repairing. God is never like that. Every one of his children is a treasured possession, worth the time and patience to mend. When the fix-it man does deem my item of sufficient value, he works miracles. With skill and patience, and with strong but gentle hands, he restores the shattered pieces into a seamless whole. The brokenness is made new. When things are going to pieces and a familiar and cherished pattern is falling apart, we must trust that God is creating a new design. These fragmented pieces of our lives have potential and possibility as he reshapes us into something again beautiful and useful, never removing his hand in the process.

As the World Turns was a good title for a daily television soap opera. How do we deal with this rotating, turning, changing life? Only by clinging to the truth that "There is no shadow of turning with God. He changest not . . . As he hast been, he forever will be."[98] The turning of the earth on its axis gives us the seasons we love. A dusting of snow will soon be followed by the scent of mountain laurel blossoms that announce the season of spring. And it is the turning points of our lives that create the ever-evolving seasons of our own lives. Remember the lesson of the kaleidoscope, a symbol of changing patterns and designs—the beauty of something new and different, as we rotate the cylinder in our hands. The kaleidoscope reminds us to trust God enough to accept change, even when it is unwelcome, because our turning world is held in his loving hands.

The book of Ecclesiastes gives us encouragement to be content in the changing seasons of our lives because "there is a time for everything":

> a time to be born and a time to die,
> a time to plant and a time to uproot,
> a time to kill and a time to heal,
> a time to tear down and a time to build,
> a time to weep and a time to laugh,
> a time to mourn and a time to dance,
> a time to scatter stones and a time to gather them,
> a time to embrace and a time to refrain from
>   embracing,
> a time to search and a time to give up,
> a time to keep and a time to throw away,
> a time to tear and a time to mend,
> a time to be silent and a time to speak, a time to
>   love and a time to hate,
> a time for war and a time for peace.

As so many have sung, "Turn! Turn! Turn! (To Everything There Is a Season)."[99]

PRAYER

We may be in a pattern of our life that we love and don't want to change. We want it to be the same in the next hour, the next week, forever. Or our life may be too static, too predictable, and we wish we could turn it into something new. Some of us may wish we could reverse the motion and go back to a happier, easier time. Let us find comfort in knowing that God is gathering all the pieces of our lives—the bright, the dark, the smooth, and the rough. Like the potter, he gathers the ones we would like to sweep under the carpet or throw in the trash as rubbish. Just as the bits of mirror, glass, and plastic have beauty only as they are contained within the kaleidoscope, so it is only in God's hands that our brokenness has potential and possibility.

THIRTY-SIX

THE HEARTBEAT OF GOD

I have loved you with an everlasting love.
—Jeremiah 31:3

Love in the prime not yet I understand—
Scarce know the love that loveth at first hand.
—George MacDonald [100]

An old Irishman and his nephew were watching a sunrise one morning. Suddenly, eighty-five-year-old Uncle Seamus began skipping down the road. When the younger man caught up with his uncle, he asked, "Why are you so happy?" "Well, laddie," replied the old man, "the Father is very fond of me!"

The apostle John felt the same way. Because God's love was his core identity, he unabashedly described himself as "the disciple whom Jesus loved" (Jn.13:23). After reclining against Jesus at the Last Supper, intimate enough to feel he was hearing the heartbeat of God, he grasped the truth that God loves with a "magnificent monotony," [101] a love that is constant and consistent.

Theologically, we know God loves us, but do we believe that he likes us? Do we know his love as deeply as Uncle Seamus and the apostle John, both of whom were "rooted and established in love"? (Eph. 3:17). Do we understand this love that "surpasses knowledge" (Eph. 3:19) so that it affects how we live, how we forgive, how we handle suffering and failure? Like John, we need to hear the heartbeat of the Father, so at every sunrise we might say, "The Father is very fond of me . . . I am the one he loves."

Although many Christian writers have addressed the theme of God's love, Dr. A. W. Tozer in *The Knowledge of the Holy* feels it is a difficult task, saying he could "no more do justice to that awesome and wonder-filled theme than a child can grasp a star." Brennan Manning believes that we need a deep awareness of Jesus' love even though we cannot earn or deserve it. We should, therefore, "define ourselves radically as the beloved of God" and know that "we ravish his heart."[102]

The revelation of God's love in his Word is beautifully expressed by Anna B. Warner in a poem she wrote in 1860, saying "Yes, Jesus loves me, the Bible tells me so." Jesus' compassion, healing, teaching, death, and resurrection demonstrate "how wide and long and high and deep is the love of Christ" (Eph. 3:18), a love from which we cannot be separated, a love that is eternal, steadfast, and unchanging.

In addition to the Bible and Christian writers, great literature can present us with a story or character that portrays a spiritual truth in a way that penetrates our souls. As the saying goes, "Truth is stranger than fiction." I believe that fiction can reveal deep truth.

In *David Copperfield*, Charles Dickens, a devout Christian, created the character of Mr. Peggotty, whose fatherly love for his adopted niece is a picture of God's intense and enduring love for each of us. Little Em'ly's home was a safe haven where she was cherished and protected by her devoted uncle who had raised her from her infancy. When she was a young woman with a job, she was guided home in the evening by a candle he placed in the window. She always knew "there's home and my uncle is there, always expecting me."

Their happy lives, however, changed dramatically when Davy invited his friend, the charming and handsome Steerforth, to Yarmouth. He quickly discovered Em'ly's beauty and began deceiving her with promises of seeing the world and becoming a lady. When she decides to run away and turn her back on home, she knows she will break her uncle's heart.

The poignant and painful scene when Mr. Peggotty learns of Little Em'ly's flight with Steerforth will bring tears to the eyes of any reader. After a sleepless night struggling with his anger and a desire for revenge, Mr. Peggotty commits himself to a single-minded quest, his "dooty" to find his niece. Sacrificing family, home, and livelihood, and faced with much hardship, the solitary figure toiled on. "I'm a' going to seek my niece," he tells Davy, "fur and wide, everywhere. I'm a' going to seek her through the world. I'm a' going to find my poor niece in her shame and bring her back."

Before departing, Mr. Peggotty instructed his sister to place a candle in the window every night so that if ever Little Em'ly should see it, it would say to her: "Come back, my child, come back. Maybe my fallen child will take heart to creep in, trembling and might come to be laid down in her old bed and rest her weary head where it was once so gay." He wanted her to know that "my unchanged love is with my darling child and I forgive her." After years of traveling the world seeking her, Mr. Peggotty finally found Little Em'ly, brought her home to Yarmouth, and then moved with her to Australia, to give her a chance for a new life.

Dickens' portrait of Mr. Peggotty's love for Little Em'ly is an allegory with a strong resemblance to Jesus' parable of the father's love for his prodigal son. It is a picture of the heavenly Father's love for us, his adopted children. His is a sacrificial love, a determined and persevering love. Because the Father's heart is bound to us forever, his love is not altered when we sin. God waits for us to come home. He waits patiently, but not passively. "The Hound of Heaven," as Francis Thompson calls him in his poem of the same name, seeks us when we "rise on the wings of the dawn [and] settle on the far side of the sea" (Ps. 139:9). He will not rest; he will not stop in his pursuit of his lost child.

The door is never locked, and the candle still burns in the window. His offer of a second chance is never tainted with judgment or condemnation.

Do we have something in common with Little Em'ly? We have our own departures, our temporary leavings from the love of the Father. We leave home for greener pastures, thinking we can find happiness and purpose apart from him. When we are deceived by other loves that seem to promise something more exciting, we may even lose our desire for home. Like Little Em'ly, we may feel that we have traveled so far from home that we can't find our way back, perhaps feeling unworthy even to be welcomed back. We need to understand that at the end of our wanderings, the arms of the Father are waiting to welcome us. He continues to say "come home, my unchanged love is with my darling child."

When we get to heaven, God may ask us only one question: "Did you know how much I loved you?" Just as the seventeenth-century monk Brother Lawrence had to practice experiencing the presence of God, so we might need to practice feeling the love of God. To find your way back home to the heart of the Father you might try these simple disciplines.

Imagine yourself leaning your head on the breast of Christ, listening for the heartbeat of God. It beats furiously, with no skipped beats, no arrhythmia. The heart-beat of God is constant, eternal, and steadfast. When we break God's heart by wandering from our true home, his heart keeps beating for his lost children. Since his love is passionate, never passive, always pursuing, we can always return home. The candle always burns in the window.

Just as the sunrise inspired Uncle Seamus to remember God's fondness for him, "let the morning bring me word of your unfailing love" (Ps. 143:8). An early morning discipline is helping me to practice living in the daily knowledge of his love. As I awaken to the sound of the 5:30 a.m. cannon at Fort Sam Houston in San Antonio and hear the first coo of the mourning dove, as I smell the aroma of coffee and feel my dog lick my cheek, my first thought is, "I am the one Jesus loves."

Following the pattern of Psalm 136, write a short summary of the significant events of your life, the good and bad, and conclude each sentence with "his steadfast love endures forever."

With a little practice in meditating on God's love for us, when we get to heaven and God asks, "Did you know how much I loved you?" We can answer with an emphatic, "Yes!"

PRAYER

Father, we pray for your lost children: For those who have known your love, but have left it for a while. Give them the desire for home, the assurance that the door is never locked, that the light is still in the window, leading them home. For those who have never known your love—that they would open the door to your knocking and invite you into their heart. For those who feel that their sin and guilt prevent them from coming home, let them hear your words: "Come back, my child, come back."

THIRTY-SEVEN

THE POPE'S CEILING

Therefore, if anyone is in Christ, the new creation has come:
the old has gone, the new is here!
—2 Corinthians 5:17

Many of you have visited the Sistine Chapel in Rome. Begun in 1477, it was designed architecturally to have the exact proportions as the Temple of Solomon in Jerusalem. The frescoes of the vaulted ceiling, painted by a team of Italian artists that included Michelangelo, took five years to complete and are the most well-known example of this remarkable and challenging art form.

In Glendale Springs, North Carolina, are two small churches with fresco paintings by Ben Long, an American artist who studied fresco painting in Italy and returned home to paint frescoes in the remote Blue Ridge Mountains of North Carolina. His frescoes don't bear much similarity to the Sistine Chapel; in fact, the models for Long's most notable fresco, "The Last Supper," were local men, ninth-generation mountaineers.

After visiting these tiny rural churches, I read *The Pope's Ceiling* by Ross King, which tells the story of Michelangelo painting the vaulted ceiling of the Sistine Chapel. When I finished the book, I realized I had written "Spiritual!" in the margin of many pages.

Fresco painting is a tricky and formidable art form that taxed even the ingenuity of Leonardo da Vinci. While many painters could succeed in tempura and oil, only a few were able to triumph in the difficult medium of fresco painting. It required that the artist be manly and resolute, made of the "sternest stuff." In comparison, tempura was seen as the domain of "effeminate young men."

When a new fresco replaces an existing one, the old fresco has to be chiseled and hacked away. The preparation for Michelangelo's work required the destruction of a beautiful bright blue heaven sprinkled with gold stars. Certainly there were people who lamented the change to something new and unfamiliar. The execution of the work can be frustrating. The word *fresco* means fresh, indicating that the plaster must be a wet, permeable surface capable of absorbing and sealing the pigments. Because the plaster dries in twelve to twenty-four hours, the artist is working against time. If the plaster becomes hard, a new coat must be applied and the artist has to start over. Therefore, the vault of the ceiling is divided into sections, each called a *giornata*, the work that can be accomplished in the span of one day. An outline of the daily section is drawn on a large sheet of paper called the cartoon. The lines of the drawing are perforated with thousands of small holes through which a charcoal powder is sprinkled, thus imprinting on the plaster an outline that the artist then reinforces in paint.

I was beginning to understand why I had seen spiritual red flags while reading *The Pope's Ceiling*. The medium is difficult, preparation is required, and the work must be accomplished in daily segments. The artist needs a certain temperament, specific skills, and technique.

God's artistry is confirmed in nature—bumblebees, butterflies, wildflowers, and thunderstorms. Just as the daunting task of the Sistine Chapel required certain characteristics of Michelangelo in order to complete his masterpiece, God has the strength, perseverance, resolve, and vision to complete the work he has begun in each of us.

Like Michelangelo, God is working with a medium that is challenging and frustrating. As his chosen art form, we will strain his patience. The myriad obstacles in fresco painting are reflected in the expression *stare fresco,* meaning to be in a fix or a mess. Could that mean us? John Ortberg comments that even the greats of the Old Testament—Solomon, Saul, and David—have been called shipwrecks.

In the process of making all things new, God might need to chip away some of our old habits and attitudes to prepare for a new work in our lives. The existing ceiling of the Sistine Chapel, the starry heavenly motif, had to be removed to make way for something even more beautiful. In the same way, things in our lives that appear good might need to be replaced by something better. The process of transformation is not easy; it is sometimes painful.

God has drawn the cartoon, a master plan, and design for our lives. "For I know the plans I have for you . . . plans to prosper you and not to harm you, plans to give you hope and a future" (Jer. 29:11). God has drawn boundary lines intended for our protection and happiness. But we are often like the stubborn child who breaks the cardinal rule of kindergarten—DO NOT color outside the lines. In pride, arrogance, and independence, we sometimes take the brush out of God's hand, thinking we can do a better job. We need to trust that it is within his outline, his plan and purpose, that vibrant color is being added to our lives—daily.

The main insight I learned from fresco painting is this: Michelangelo knew the master design when he began his work, just as God knows his design for our lives. But great work on a masterpiece—by Michelangelo or by God—is done in daily segments. God used a sunrise to remind me that each day is a gift and an opportunity. I awoke to see streaks of pink and orange on the horizon. As the sun rose in the summer sky, the fiery ball created a column of shimmering red in the water of the lake. It looked like an inverted exclamation mark (¡). This is God's attitude about how we should greet each new day. It reminded me that every day is the day the Lord has made! Let us rejoice and be glad in it! (Ps. 118:24). Every day offers blessings and challenges that add color to our lives. Every day, God is working on his masterpiece—your life and mine.

PRAYER

Father, you are the Artist with a vision and plan for your completed work. You are committed to transforming our lives into something that reflects your handiwork. Let us join you in this process, offering hearts that are willing to replace old patterns with something that is new and better. We want to keep our hearts soft and pliable by being in your Word, by prayer and worship, so we can absorb and then seal your love, teaching, and guidance. We remember the words of Genesis: on the first day, on the second day, the third day . . . Giornata by giornata the earth was created. Day by day, you are chipping away the old to create something new in our lives. Help us daily to discern your plans, knowing you have designed us to be a vibrant reflection of your Son.

THIRTY-EIGHT

FLOWERS IN THE CEMETERY

'What no eye has seen, what no ear has heard,
and what no human mind has conceived'—
the things God has prepared for those who love him—
—1 Corinthians 2:9

On a driving trip in Switzerland, John and I stopped to admire a charming cemetery of simple wooden crosses amidst a profusion of flowers. Each cross bears the name of the deceased, the year of birth and the year of death. In the front of my Bible, I keep one of the photographs I took that day.

Maria Elena was born in 1948. Because I was born the same year, I was curious. I wanted to know how old she was when she died, but vibrant and colorful flowers obscure the part of the cross with the year of her death. Did she die as a child leaving her parents heartbroken? Perhaps she was a young wife. Has her husband remarried? Do her children think of her often? She must have loved animals because a ceramic fawn is nestled among the blooms surrounding her grave. Did she die of cancer? A childhood illness? A car accident on the mountain road? The care that has been given to beautify her grave is testimony that she was well loved and is still remembered.

Although I will never know the date of Maria Elena's death, I certainly remember the days and years when my loved ones have died. We can all share stories of the circumstances surrounding these times. When death has come suddenly or to a young person, the stories are tragic. Other stories are about parents or grandparents who died peacefully after living a long life.

Paul poses the question, "Where, O death, is your victory? Where, O death, is your sting?" (1 Cor. 15:55). The death of a loved one does sting! But because of Jesus' resurrection, death does not have the last word. Death is covered by a riot of flowers in every color of the rainbow, flowers that thrive and flourish because they are planted close to the cross. Sitting outside one morning in the Blue Ridge Mountains, overwhelmed by the beauty of God's creation and feeling deep contentment and gratitude, I thought, "It just doesn't get any better than this." My Bible opened to 1 Corinthians 2:9, "No eye has seen, no ear has heard, no human heart has conceived what God has prepared for those who love him." Yes, it does get better than this!

When I look at the photograph of Maria Elena's grave, I am reminded that none of us knows when death will come. I say a prayer for her family and then I say a prayer of gratitude for the gift of another day in this life. And I resolve not to be "held in slavery by . . . fear of death" (Heb. 2:15), the when and how of my own passing or that of my loved ones. Because Jesus is my light and salvation, the stronghold of my life, I should not be afraid. We understand the meaning of the cross: Jesus has "tasted death for everyone" (Heb. 2:9). We understand the meaning of the empty tomb: "Death has been swallowed up in victory." (1 Cor. 15:54).

If we can grasp the magnitude of God's love for us, our fear of death should diminish. Because of his great love for his children, he has prepared eternity to be something beyond what we can imagine. When we see a crucifix, we should know that God loves like that. And he does!

We consider "love" to be a simple word. But, in fact, it always needs a dictionary, the dictionary that is Jesus Christ himself. "He took this chameleon of a word and gave it a fast colour, so that ever since it is lustred by His teaching and life, and dyed in the crimson of Calvary, and shot through with the sunlight of Easter morning."[103] We are rooted in the love of Christ, a love that is wide and long and high and deep.

Jesus' love was so wide that it recognized no boundary of class, culture, ethnicity, nationality, or gender. In contrast, our natures are "capable of deep affection for one person or a few . . . apt to build a wall round the field of our narrowly exercised affections."[104] When you are flying to England, and your plane begins its descent, you see green fields bordered and enclosed by ancient stone walls and hedgerows, each field containing a scattering of sheep owned by one person. My love for others is often like that—sturdy boundaries that admit only a few close friends and family. Occasionally, the gate will open to let someone else in. The field of Jesus' love has a gate that is always open.

Jesus' love for us is deep. It does not turn away at our sin but continues to pursue us when we wander. How deep is our love for our neighbor? It is not difficult to love up to a point—"the point where my neighbor . . . turns out to be less attractive than he seemed at first blush, to be difficult, or a regular twister, or perhaps just a bore."[105] But then we draw the line. To grasp the depth of Jesus' love for sinners, imagine a beach full of refuse at the end of a holiday weekend. Returning the next morning, we wonder: "Where is all the trash that had accumulated?" It appears that the steady and strong force of the wind and waves have accomplished the daunting task of cleaning the beach overnight. In the same way that the stain of sin in our lives is swept clean by wave upon wave of God's grace, the constant cleansing current of his love that washes over us.

Rod Stewart sings of the height of God's love: "Your love keeps liftin' me higher than I've ever been lifted before." When we are downhearted and disappointed we can discover the lifting love of Jesus. No matter how far we fall or for what reason, the love, mercy, and forgiveness of our Savior will lift us.

And the length of God's love? As long as eternity.

The comfort and assurance for us is not just that God loves humankind, but that he loves each of us in a personal and intimate way. We are not a faceless mass of children or friends but known individually by the Creator of the universe. A missionary in Canada conveyed this important lesson to a frail, ill child. He taught the boy "The Lord is my Shepherd"—five words, one for each finger of the boy's small hand. He encouraged the boy to always hold on to the fourth finger, corresponding with the word *my*. A year later, when the missionary returned to the same village, he learned that the child had died. The parents found him one morning, his hands outside the coverlet, his left hand clasped around the fourth finger of his right hand.[106]

There are flowers in the graveyard. Death is covered over by vibrant life. Look at the cross and know, this is how much he loves you. His is a love that searches far and wide for people to bring into his fold, a love that washes away our sins, a love that raises us to safe heights when we have fallen, and a love whose length we cannot fathom.

He is my Shepherd. He is your Shepherd.

PRAYER

Father, you know the truth. We do fear death. We dread the sting of losing a loved one. But we trust that we will "dwell in the house of the Lord all the days of [our] life" (Ps. 27:4), now in this earthly life and in eternity. Your hold on us is strong, both sides of the grave. Let us ponder the four points of the cross as a reminder of the height, depth, width, and length of your love. We behold the cross and we know "God loves like that!"

ACKNOWLEDGMENTS

I wish to express my gratitude:

For God's propensity to choose unlikely people to serve him. As I dropped every course in college that required an oral report, he knew that forty years later, I would be speaking in front of a group of fifty women, giving talks about faith. When God moves you out of your comfort zone to serve him in a way you never imagined, there are blessings to be found.

For those who talked to me about their faith long before I was ready to accept or understand. The seeds they planted finally blossomed into a faith of my own.

For Bible study leaders who nourished and encouraged me, especially Sissy Orsinger, who shared her devotion to studying God's Word and her passion for prayer.

For my pastor (now retired) and friend, Louis Zbinden, whose teaching and preaching gave a foundation for my developing faith. It was his sermon about being "F.A.T." for God (faithful, available, and teachable) that gave me the courage to become a small group leader of Bible studies.

For the ladies with whom I have studied the Bible over the years. They have enriched my life and taught me so much. We have been each other's village as we have faced the challenges of raising children and taking care of aging parents. We have prayed for and encouraged each other as we have faced the joys and struggles of life.

For my neighbor and friend Gail Smith, who opened her home for seven years, welcoming us every Monday.

For the other leaders who were instrumental in helping this group to thrive and stay organized: Janie Worth, Cynthia McMurray, Bebe Gorman, Kathey Anderson, Carolyn Johnson, and the late Glenda Woods.

For Leah Lowrey's invaluable assistance in getting the manuscript and photographs ready for publication. In the countless hours we worked together, her sweet spirit encouraged me to stay on task and bring this project to completion.

For my precious husband, John, whose opinion I value above all others. From the beginning, he was the sounding board for my ideas. Many Sunday lunches were spent discussing the "fireside chat" to be presented to the group on Monday. He supported me and assured me that it was worth the time and effort to turn these talks into a manuscript. As a writer, he was my first editor—patient with my spelling and creative punctuation. Mainly I am so grateful that he believed in me and made me finish!

NOTES

LIMOGES BOXES
1.   MacDonald, George, *A Book of Strife in the Form of The Diary of an Old Soul* (1880), courtesy of Project Gutenberg, www.gutenberg.org.
2   MacDonald, *A Book of Strife.*
3   Peterson, Eugene H., *Run with the Horses: The Quest for Life at Its Best* (IVP Books, 2010), p.16.

THE TOUCH OF GRACE
4   Baker, Henry W., *"The King of Love My Shepherd Is"* (1868).
5   McGee, J. Vernon, *Thru the Bible, Commentary vol. 54: The Epistles: (1 Peter)* (Thomas Nelson, 1995).

CLOUDS' ILLUSIONS
6   Sandburg, Carl, *The Complete Poems of Carl Sandburg: Revised and Expanded Edition* (Harcourt, Brace and Co. 1916), p.33.
7   Anonymous fourteenth-century English writer, Translated by A. C. Spearing, *The Cloud of Unknowing and Other Works* (2001).
8   Robinson, Robert, "Come Thou Fount of Every Blessing" (1757).

THE L'IMITATION OF GOD
9   Moore, Clement Clarke, "'Twas the Night Before Christmas," courtesy of Project Gutenberg, www.gutenberg.org.
10   Thoreau, Henry David, *Excursions and Poems* (1865), courtesy of Project Gutenberg, www.gutenberg.org.

THE WALLS OF LUCCA
11   Lucado, Max, *Grace for the Moment, Volume II: More Inspirational Thoughts for Each Day of the Year* (Thomas Nelson, 2006).

12   Thomas, Gary, *Seeking the Face of God: The Path to A More Intimate Relationship* (Harvest House Publishers, 1999), p. 122.

IN THE LAND OF COUNTERPANE
13   Wiederkehr, Macrina, *A Tree Full of Angels: Seeing the Holy in the Ordinary* (HarperOne, 2009), p. xiii, xiv.
14   Wiederkehr, *A Tree Full of Angels*, p. xiii.
15   Perks, Bob, "I Wish You Enough!®" iwishyouenough. com, accessed April 29, 2013.

SNAPSHOTS OF THE SAVIOR
16   Voskamp, Ann, *One Thousand Gifts: A Dare to Live Fully Right Where You Are* (Zondervan, 2011), p. 74.
17   Bonhoeffer, Dietrich, *God Is in the Manger: Reflections on Advent and Christmas* (Westminster John Knox Press, 2012), p. 14.
18   Nouwen, Henri, *The Dance of Life: Weaving Sorrows and Blessings into One Joyful Step* (Ave Maria Press, 2006), p. 36.

THE GOOD BOOK
19   Shaffer, Mary Ann, *The Guernsey Literary and Potato Peel Pie Society* (Dial Press, 2009), p. 63.
20   MacDonald, George, *The Heart of George MacDonald* (Regent College Publishing, 1994), p. 315.
21   Bernard of Clairvaux, "In Defense of Humility" (1120–1153).
22   Lucado, Max, *In the Grip of Grace* (Thomas Nelson, 1999), p.105.

THE LADYBUG CASTS A LONG SHADOW
23   Quindlen, Anna, *Every Last One* (Random House, 2010), p. 213.
24   Quindlen, *Every Last One*, p. 214.
25   Kleinhaus, Kathryn, "The Work of a Christian," Word & World, vol. 25, no. 4 (Word & World, Luther Seminary, Fall 2005), p. 394.
26   Kleinhaus, "The Work of a Christian," p. 394.

THE GIRL AND THE ELEPHANT
27   Gates, David, "If (Bread Song)" (1971).

WINDBLOWN
28   Foster, Richard J., *Life with God: Reading the Bible for Spiritual Transformation* (HarperOne, 2010), p. 23.
29   Walls, Jeannette, *The Glass Castle: A Memoir* (Scribner, 2006) p. 38.

30   Thoreau, *Excursions and Poems.*
31   Wright, N. T., *Acts for Everyone: Part One* (Westminster John Knox Press, 2008), p. 22.
32   Von Schlegel, Katharina A., "Be Still, My Soul" (1752); Borthwick, Jane L. Translation from German to English (1855).
33   Jeffery, George Johnstone, *The Sacramental Table: A Series of Addresses by Representative Scots Preachers* (James Clarke, 1954), p. 34.

CHARING CROSS
34   Boswell, James, *Life of Samuel Johnson* (Penguin Classics, 2008), p. 443.
35   Lucado, Max, *And the Angels Were Silent* (Thomas Nelson, 2005), p. 29.
36   Blackmur, R. P., *The Lion and the Honeycomb* (Harcourt, 1955), p. 180.

THE HEART OF THE RESCUER
37   Lyte, Henry F., "Praise My Soul the King of Heaven" (1834).
38   Jeffery, *The Sacramental Table*, p. 60.

WHERE IS WALDO?
39   Wiederkehr, *A Tree Full of Angels*, p. 83.
40   Tozer, A. W., *The Pursuit of God* (2008), courtesy of Project Gutenberg, www.gutenberg.org.

A REMODELING JOB
41   Carlson, Margaret, "Domestic Lives," *New York Times* (September 12, 2012).
42   MacDonald, *A Book of Strife.*
43   MacDonald, *A Book of Strife.*
44   Lewis, C. S., *Mere Christianity* (HarperSanFrancisco, 1980), p. 198.
45   Willard, Dallas, *Renovation of the Heart: Putting on the Character of Christ* (NavPress, 2002), p. 3.
46   Caliguire, Mindy, *Discovering Soul Care* (IVP Connect, 2007), p. 44.

FAILED DOG
47   Manning, Brennan, *The Ragamuffin Gospel* (HarperOne, 1998), p. 25.
48   Peterson, Eugene H., *Living the Resurrection: The Risen Christ in Everyday Live* (NavPress, 2006), p. 10.
49   Peterson, *Run with the Horses,* pp. 15–16.

50   Muggeridge, Malcolm, *Jesus: The Man who Lives* (HarperSanFranscisco, 1976), p. 119.
51   Peterson, *Run with the Horses,* p. 37.
52   Muggeridge, Jesus: *The Man Who Lives*, p. 120.
53   Walls, Jeannette, *Half Broke Horses* (Scribner, 2010), p. 19.

WISE GUYS
54   Hopkins, John Henry, Jr., "We Three Kings" (1857).
55   Hopkins, "We Three Kings."
56   Hopkins, "We Three Kings."
57   Caliguire, *Discovering Soul Care*, p. 15.
58   Opie, I. and P., *The Oxford Dictionary of Nursery Rhymes* (Oxford University Press,1997), p. 304.
59   Shakespeare, William, *The Complete Works of William Shakespeare*, "Sonnet No. 73" (1609), courtesy of Project Gutenberg, www.gutenberg.org.
60   Spangler, Ann, *The Names of Jesus* (Zondervan, 2006), p. 173.

GOD'S BIOGRAPHIES
61   Paine, Thomas, *The Writings of Thomas Paine—Volume 1 (1774–1779): The American Crisis* (originally published from 1776 to 1783), courtesy of Project Gutenberg, www.gutenberg.org.

HOMESICK
62   Foster, *Life with God*, p. 86.
63   MacDonald, *A Book of Strife.*
64   Smith, Walter C., "Immortal, Invisible" (1876).
65   Foster, *Life With God*, p. 86.
66   Warren, Diane, performed by Lee Ann Rimes, "How Do I Live" (1997).
67   Warren, "How Do I Live."

COFFEE WITH THE NATIVITY
68   Rosetti, Christina, "In the Bleak Midwinter" (1872).

MY PEACE I GIVE YOU
69   Stanley, Charles, *The Wonderful Spirit Filled Life* (Thomas Nelson, 1995), p. 108.

PRAISE GOD ANYWAY
70   Redman, Matt, "Blessed Be Your Name" (1999).

71   Anderson, Bernhard W., *Out of the Depths: The Psalms Speak for Us Today* (Westminster John Knox Press, 2000), p. 98.
72   Eby, J. Preston, "Teaching the Things Concerning the Kingdom of God," *The Heavens Declare*, Part 26: Sagittarius—The Archer, can be found at www.kingdombiblestudies.org/index1.htm.
73   Lewis, C. S., *A Grief Observed* (HarperOne, 2009), p. 74.
74   Lemmel, Helen, "Turn Your Eyes Upon Jesus" (1922).

WAITING
75   Lemmel, "Turn Your Eyes Upon Jesus."

TELL ME THE OLD, OLD STORY
76   Hankey, Katherine, "Tell Me the Old, Old Story" (1866).
77   Peterson, Eugene H., *Eat This Book: A Conversation in the Art of Spiritual Reading* (Wm. B. Eerdmans, 2010), p. 40.
78   Yancy, Philip, *The Jesus I Never Knew* (Zondervan, 2002), p. 289.
79   Robinson, Marilynne, *Home* (Farrar, Straus, and Giroux, 2008), p. 104.
80   Peterson, *Eat This Book,* p. 43.
81   Hall, Thelma, *Too Deep for Words* (Paulist Press, 1988), p. 9.

SEEKING THE FACE OF GOD
82   Foster, Richard J., *Celebration of Discipline: The Path to Spiritual Growth* (HarperSanFrancisco, 2002), p. 189.
83   Lemmel, "Turn Your Eyes Upon Jesus."
84   Tozer, *The Pursuit of God.*
85   Tozer, *The Pursuit of God.*
86   Tozer, *The Pursuit of God.*
87   Pitts, William, "The Church in the Wildwood" (1857).
88   Bernard of Clairvaux, translated by Edward Caswall, "Jesus the Very Thought of Thee"(1120–1153) (1849 translation).

A SPANIEL'S FALL FROM GRACE
89   Wesley, Charles, "Love Divine, All Loves Excelling" (1747).

THE QUILTS OF GEE'S BEND
90   Arnett, William; Beardsley, John; Livingston, Jane; and Wardlaw, Alvia, *The Quilts of Gee's Bend* (Tinwood Books, 2002), p. 14.

GOD'S WALKING PARTNER
91   Voskamp, *One Thousand Gifts*, p. 65.
92   Thoreau, *Excursions and Poems*.

LISTENING FOR GOD
93   Willard, Dallas, *Hearing God: Developing a Conversational Relationship with God* (IVP Books, 2012).
94   Gilbert, Elizabeth, *Eat, Pray, Love: One Woman's Search for Everything Across Italy, India and Indonesia* (Penguin Books, 2007), p. 132.
95   Gilbert, *Eat, Pray, Love*, p.142.
96   Ogilvie, Lloyd John, *Conversations with God* (Harvest House Publishers, 1998), p. 53.

THE KALEIDOSCOPE
97   Peterson, *Run with the Horses*, p. 78.
98   Chisholm, Thomas, "Great Is Thy Faithfulness" (1923).
99   Seeger, Pete (music and lyrics), and Aber, George (lyrics adaptation), "Turn! Turn! Turn! (To Everything There Is a Season)" (1959).

THE HEARTBEAT OF GOD
100   MacDonald, *A Book of Strife*.
101   Manning, *The Ragamuffin Gospel*, p. 37.
102   Manning, *The Ragamuffin Gospel*, p. 25.

FLOWERS IN THE CEMETERY
103   Jeffery, *The Sacramental Table*, p. 50.
104   Jeffery, *The Sacramental Table*, p. 50.
105   Jeffery, *The Sacramental Table*, p. 51.
106   Jeffery, *The Sacramental Table*, p. 55.

SOURCES AND SELECTIONS FOR FURTHER READING

Anderson, Bernhard W., *Out of the Depths: The Psalms Speak for Us Today* (Westminster John Knox Press, 2000).

Anonymous fourteenth-century English writer, Translated by A. C. Spearing, *The Cloud of Unknowing and Other Works* (2001).

Arnett, William; Beardsley, John; Livingston, Jane; and Wardlaw, Alvia, *The Quilts of Gee's Bend* (Tinwood Books, 2002).

Augustine, Saint, Bishop of Hippo, *Confessions* (Dover Publications, 2012).

Blackmur, R. P., *The Lion and the Honeycomb* (Harcourt, 1955).

Bonhoeffer, Dietrich, *God Is in the Manger: Reflections on Advent and Christmas* (Westminster John Knox Press, 2012).

Boswell, James, *Life of Samuel Johnson* (Penguin Classics, 2008).

Buchanan, Mark, *Things Unseen: Living in Light in Light of Forever* (Multnomah Books, 2006).

Caliguire, Mindy, *Discovering Soul Care* (IVP Connect, 2007).

Dean, Jennifer, *Secrets Jesus Shared* (New Hope Publishers, 2007).

Foster, Richard J., *Celebration of Discipline: The Path to Spiritual Growth* (HarperSanFrancisco, 2002).

Foster, Richard J., *Life with God: Reading the Bible for Spiritual Transformation* (HarperOne, 2010).

Gilbert, Elizabeth, *Eat, Pray, Love: One Woman's Search for Everything Across Italy, India and Indonesia* (Penguin Books, 2007).

Hall, Thelma, *Too Deep for Words* (Paulist Press, 1988).

Holmes, Marjorie, *Two from Galilee: The Story of Mary and Joseph* (Bantam, 1982).

Hybels, Bill, *Too Busy Not To Pray* (Intervarsity Press, 1988).

Jeffery, George Johnstone, *The Sacramental Table: A Series of Addresses by Representative Scots Preachers* (James Clarkc, 1954).

Jewette, Robert, *Saint Paul Returns to the Movies: Triumph over Shame* (Wm. B. Eerdmans, 1998).

Lawrence, Brother of the Reserrection, *The Practice of the Presence of God* (Image, 1977).

Lewis, C. S., *A Grief Observed* (HarperOne, 2009).

Lewis, C. S., *Mere Christianity* (HarperSanFrancisco, 1980).

Lucado, Max, *And the Angels Were Silent* (Thomas Nelson, 2005).

Lucado, Max, *Grace for the Moment, Volume II: More Inspirational Thoughts for Each Day of the Year* (Thomas Nelson, 2006).

Lucado, Max, *In the Grip of Grace* (Thomas Nelson, 1999).

MacDonald, George, *A Book of Strife in the Form of The Diary of an Old Soul* (1880), courtesy of Project Gutenberg, www.gutenberg.org.

MacDonald, George, *The Heart of George MacDonald* (Regent College Publishing, 1994).

Manning, Brennan, *The Ragamuffin Gospel* (HarperOne, 1998).

Marshall, Catherine, *The Helper* (Chosen Books, 2001).

McGee, J. Vernon, *Thru the Bible, Commentary, vol. 54: The Epistles: (1 Peter)* (Thomas Nelson, 1995),

Muggeridge, Malcolm, *Jesus: The Man Who Lives* (HarperSan-Franscisco, 1976).

Nouwen, Henri, *The Dance of Life: Weaving Sorrows and Blessings into One Joyful Step* (Ave Maria Press, 2006).

Ogilvie, Lloyd John, *Autobiography of God* (Regal Books, 1981).

Ogilvie, Lloyd John, *Conversations with God* (Harvest House, 1998).

Opie, I. and P., *The Oxford Dictionary of Nursery Rhymes* (Oxford University Press,1997).

Packer, J. I., *Knowing God* (InterVarsity Press, 1993).

Paine, Thomas, *The Writings of Thomas Paine—Volume 1 (1774–1779): The American Crisis* (originally published from 1776 to 1783), courtesy of Project Gutenberg, www.gutenberg.org.

Peterson, Eugene H., *Eat This Book: A Conversation in the Art of Spiritual Reading* (Wm. B. Eerdmans, 2010).

Peterson, Eugene H., *Living the Resurrection: The Risen Christ in Everyday Live* (NavPress, 2006).

Peterson, Eugene H., *A Long Obedience in the Same Direction: Discipleship in an Instant Society* (Intervarsity Press, 1980).

Peterson, Eugene H., *Run with the Horses: The Quest for Life at Its Best* (IVP Books, 2010).

Quindlen, Anna, *Every Last One* (Random House, 2010).

Robinson, Marilynne, *Home* (Farrar, Straus, and Giroux, 2008).

Rosetti, Christina, "In the Bleak Midwinter" (1872).

Sandburg, Carl, "Fog" (1916).

Shaffer, Mary Ann, *The Guernsey Literary and Potato Peel Pie Society* (Dial Press, 2009).

Spangler, Ann, *Praying the Names of Jesus: A Daily Guide* (Zondervan, 2006).

Stanley, Charles F., *The Wonderful Spirit Filled Life* (Thomas Nelson, 1995).

Thomas, Gary, *Seeking the Face of God: The Path to A More Intimate Relationship* (Harvest House Publishers, 1999).

Thoreau, Henry David, *Excursions and Poems* (1865), courtesy of Project Gutenberg, www.gutenberg.org.

Tozer, A. W., *The Pursuit of God* (2008), courtesy of Project Gutenberg, www.gutenberg.org.

Vanauken, Sheldon, *A Severe Mercy* (HarperOne, 2009).

Voskamp, Ann, *One Thousand Gifts: A Dare to Live Fully Right Where You Are* (Zondervan, 2011).

Willard, Dallas, *Hearing God: Developing a Conversational Relationship with God* (IVP Books, 2012).

Willard, Dallas, *Renovation of the Heart: Putting on the Character of Christ* (NavPress, 2002).

Wiederkehr, Macrina, *A Tree Full of Angels: Seeing the Holy in the Ordinary* (HarperOne, 2009).

Wright, N. T., *Acts for Everyone: Part One* (Westminster John Knox Press, 2008).

Yancy, Philip, *The Jesus I Never Knew* (Zondervan, 2002).

Yancy, Philip, *Prayer, Does it Make Any Difference?* (Zondervan, 2006).

Yancy, Philip, *What's So Amazing About Grace?* (Zondervan, 2008).

INDEX BY THEME

God Calls Us Home

God's Abundance

We Seek God

We Pray

We Trust God

We Worship God

We Know God

We Serve God